The

Summer Kitchen

Books by Louise Andrews Kent

The Terrace
Paul Revere Square
Mrs. Appleyard's Year
Mrs. Appleyard's Kitchen
Country Mouse
". . . with Kitchen Privileges"
The Summer Kitchen
(with Elizabeth Kent Gay)
The Winter Kitchen
(with Elizabeth Kent Gay)

Stories for Young People

Douglas of Porcupine
The Red Rajah
Two Children of Tyre
He Went with Marco Polo
He Went with Vasco da Gama
He Went with Magellan
He Went with Christopher Columbus
Jo Ann, Tomboy (with Ellis Parker Butler)
In Good Old Colony Times
(with Elizabeth Kent Tarshis)
The Brookline Trunk
He Went with John Paul Jones
He Went with Champlain
He Went with Drake

By Elizabeth Kent Tarshis

The Village that Learned to Read

Mrs. Appleyard's Summer Kitchen

LOUISE ANDREWS KENT
AND
ELIZABETH KENT GAY

DECORATIONS BY JOHN O'HARA COSGRAVE II

Keats Publishing, Inc. New Canaan, Connecticut

For
JOHN TREVILLE LATOUCHE
one of whose many kindnesses to the authors
was reading the manuscript of this book

Contents

Contents

NOTE

* Indicates recipes printed in this book.
† Those found in Mrs. Appleyard's Kitchen.
‡ In ". . . with Kitchen Privileges."

The
Summer Kitchen

The Summer Kitchen

Iᴛ's ᴀʙᴏᴜᴛ ᴛɪᴍᴇ," Cicely Bradshaw said to her mother, "that you wrote another cookbook."

Mrs. Appleyard — for it was she — briskly swept her new car around one of those reverse curves so dear to the hearts of Vermont road builders, reached into her pocketbook and handed her eldest daughter a rather weary-looking pencil. Also an envelope kindly contributed by a grower of Dutch bulbs.

"You write it," she said firmly.

From these few words there developed a contest of wits and wills to see which of these strong but amiable characters would do the writing and which would read over the manuscript and say: "That's fine, splendid, just what I had in mind — but did it ever occur to you . . ."

On the first day, however, everything went serenely. This was partly because Mrs. Appleyard was driving and had therefore automatically won the first round. Also, the first hint of a new book is like the scent of boiling coffee or the smell of a new car — a fragrance all the more exciting because you know it will never be quite realized. What coffee ever tasted the way it smells? What car ever quite became the magic carpet implied by the aroma wafted out as you opened the door for your first drive? What book — ?

Still, as Cicely pointed out, September is a good time for new enterprises.

"Think of all the parties we've been to and the different menus and the remarkable people we know. We'll put them all in," she said.

"Perhaps we had better not," her mother said cautiously.

Cicely had been reading Harriet Wilson's memoirs. She suggested that they might imitate that lady and ask people how much they would pay to have their names left out.

"An excellent idea," Mrs. Appleyard said. "I leave the negotiations entirely to you. Somehow I don't feel that blackmail is one of my talents . . . Which of these roads would you advise me to take? They both seem to have a good deal of grass growing down the middle."

They chose the left fork, which ended in the dooryard of a farm. Hillcrest View Farm it was called. It had a fine collection of barns carefully placed so as to shut out a Grade A Vermont view from the house. They tried the right fork. It led up to a camp covered with imitation brick siding. A sign said "Reduce Speed. Men Drinking."

The view in this case was obscured by another camp, also covered with an imitation of one of the uglier styles of brick and cowering under a collection of paper clips and old hairpins which suggested that the cultural advantages of television were available to the inhabitants. The name of the camp was "Duneatin."

"Very appropriate," said Cicely looking sternly at her mother. "After today's menu I wonder we dare write a cookbook."

Mrs. Appleyard was seen to blush. It was she who had provided the materials for the picnic lunch from her freezer. She had, she confessed, forgotten that it took longer to thaw things out in October than it did in June. The Pepperidge Farm bread came in chilled slices more suitable for shingling a roof than for making sandwiches. The stick of unsalted butter resisted the knife to the last. A small jar of pâté would have made a good billiard ball.

Choosing a picnic spot is always difficult when more than one person is involved. The compromise on this particular day was in a dark and chilly "gulf" — Vermont for wooded glen — through which the wind beat steadily. The picnic table stood beside a rocky stream; its benches creaked perilously. To finish off this arctic meal a small can of frozen orange juice had been provided; luckily the can opener was missing.

"It is possible," said Mrs. Appleyard calmly, "that the season for picnics is over.

"Vermonters certainly have a great natural talent for ugliness," she added. "I suppose it's a reaction from living in the most beautiful place in the world."

"No doubt it's annoying to have to see all those colors," Cicely agreed.

Indeed there was a wide variety of colors to dislike. The

leaves turned early that September, turned without a touch of frost. No leaves had yet been burned brown, but had ripened in sunshine to their full brilliance. Wind and rain had carried none away. The maples shone under the blue and silver sky in shades of crimson and maroon, in scarlet, apricot and rose, in orange, yellow and dull gold, in pale green tipped with coral. Steeple firs were dark accents among them. Larches were changing from green to bronze. Ash leaves were yellow stained with purple, beech leaves yellow and russet. Discs of gold and silver quivered on birches and poplars.

The lakes were dark steel-gray mirrors that day. Hardly a ripple broke the reflections of the hills. Clouds drifted slowly across the sun, making deep purple shadows on the lion-colored mountaintops. Fields were still as green as Vermont fields in May. It was, in short, just an average autumn day, a suitable day for the 251 Club to inspect the country.

This Vermont club consists of people who have visited or intended to visit all the two hundred and fifty-one towns in the state. Mrs. Appleyard and her daughter have already colored in more than half the towns on their map. Cicely's daughter Camilla is also a member. Luckily she is a child who resembles her mother and grandmother in that she "likes to go." This is one of the most damaging things one Vermont woman can say about another. If you want to be equally scathing about a man you say he is "moderate." Well, at least no one in the Appleyard family is moderate. Cicely and her mother have attacked the 251 Club project with their usual spirit.

"We are writing our book," they now say every day as they start down the road in a cloud of dust. "Back at six." Even Tommy Bradshaw, an earnest advocate of the theory that mothers and grandmothers ought to stay at home while boys and men are out in the woods with guns, accepts this excuse. He realizes that interesting meals result from such a project.

However, it was in a tone with a slight edge of suspicion that he inquired, "What is the name of this book?"

"*The Summer Kitchen*," his mother replied glibly.

Tommy stirred the pound of sausage he was cooking for a light lunch for himself and asked, "Why?"

Because — his mother told him — we are writing about the things people like to eat in the summer, especially at parties. You know how in all the houses around here people have two kitchens, a cool airy one for summer and a warm crowded one for winter. You can't have a hundred people to supper so easily in the winter but you can in the summertime.

"I like both Grandma's kitchens," Tommy said. "The summer one is nice and cool, all green and white. I like Beatrice Duncan's picture of the old dance hall. But I like the winter kitchen best, with a fire in the wood stove, cake in the oven, steak in the broiler, oatmeal cookies in the red tin box. Gosh, I'm hungry. So why won't you write about winter?"

"This book," his mother said firmly, "is about summer. Your grandmother planned it that way."

"Cicely," Mrs. Appleyard was saying at about the same time, "feels that this ought to be a summer cookbook — full of useful hints about what you serve when a poet and two composers and a subsistence farmer drop in for a game of croquet. Or what to do when a playwright lays the beet greens he is cutting up on your great-grandmother's needlepoint chair. It ought to be a practical book, she says."

So, happily supplying alibis for each other, these writers began work on *The Summer Kitchen*.

May

Ordeal by Birthday

CICELY BRADSHAW was up attic, sorting out old snapshots. Having decided that morning to give a large party the following Saturday, she naturally began her housecleaning and general preparations at the point farthest removed from the part of the house normally seen by guests. Whether she would get the kitchen floor mopped, the table set and her dress on in time for the arrival of the guests was another matter; at least she would be clothed in a virtuous glow and the knowledge that the garage was in perfect order.

A birthday was a fine excuse for a party, thought Cicely,

but this year she would not announce the reason for her celebration. The debris of her own life and that of many other
people lay about her in the dusty sunlight of the shed chamber,
and she emphatically did not wish for more things to look
after, to keep in good repair, to make decisions about and to
shove up attic when their usefulness was past. She had not
the character to take these cast-offs to the dump, and she
clung to the New England principle that each discarded treasure would one day come in handy again. This happened just
often enough to confirm her in her squirreling ways.

Camilla, her youngest child, and the only one not at school,
had draped herself in a bedraggled boa of lavender feathers
and was trying on a green glass lampshade for a hat.

"Give me that," said her mother briskly. "It's just the thing
for Geoffrey Toussaint's housewarming present. I hate it
and he will adore it and we shall both be happy."

She stopped her trancelike absorption in the box of snapshots
and set to repairing the lampshade with that characteristic
rapidity of motion which often terrified those who usually saw
her in a state of amiable lethargy. People did not realize, Cicely
had to explain, that this was the way most Vermonters did
their work, and that the leaning against farm buildings and the
propping up by shovels and rakes was simply the gathering of
energy for the most economical use of muscle and sinew.

As she worked, the menu for the party began to arrange itself in her mind, for she was blessed with the capacity of visual-
izing in full color and three dimensions.

It would undoubtedly be a cold evening, she decided, just
right for hot spiced tomato juice, with a dash of rose hips for
Geoffrey's sake. Mrs. Appleyard's cheese biscuits to go with
it, cut in small fancy shapes. Then veal cut in small squares,

pounded flat, lined with prosciutto and filled with parsley, garlic and lemon, finely chopped, the whole thing pinned together and braised in a white wine sauce; with the veal, green peppers Wellfleet, lightly cooked and marinated, and a salad of avocado, grapefruit and orange sections with watercress; for dessert her specialty, a many-layered meringue torte, chocolate filled and whipped-cream decorated.

Cicely found her imagination so compelling that even though it was only eleven-thirty she couldn't wait for lunch. She and Camilla abandoned their housecleaning in favor of scrambled eggs unusually ambrosial.

By the end of the week the cleaning-up process had wound its way through the upstairs and the less prominent portion of the downstairs. Cicely was calm in the knowledge that her closets were tidy, her desk drawers in order and that she had found a number of items missing since Christmas, including the belt to her best dress. The green peppers were marinating in their garlic-laden dressing, the veal had been pounded and stuffed and the mocha torte mellowed in the refrigerator; by Saturday afternoon Cicely had got round to laying out silver and napkins, in between sliding pans of cheese biscuits in and out of the oven.

Having sent the children off in all directions to spend the night with patient friends, Cicely settled down to the final marshaling of forces. From childhood she had been one of those who likes to eat a little bit of everything on her plate so that the last forkful contains nicely balanced portions of meat, vegetable and gravy. So she now enjoyed bringing the various elements of the party to a climax. The meal was almost ready now, timed to give leeway for the almost certain late arrival of at least one third of the guests. The fire was laid with white birch logs and the first footstep on the porch would be the signal for lighting it. Cicely had been able to change her clothes and do her hair. What could go wrong?

That something would go wrong was the lesson that Cicely had learned through long experience. The departure of the children had eliminated four possible disaster areas — they could neither make demands on her nor attack each other at a critical moment. She would not be called away to serve drinks of water, admire a new hairdo, observe the charm of a repeating cap pistol, find a lost arithmetic book. As she set the plates to warm and the water pitcher to chill, she reviewed all the possible catastrophes, feeling that this gave her some power over them. Short of a tornado the electricity should stay on through the evening. The gas tank was a fresh one and couldn't give out during the final cooking; the furnace would hardly be needed, but if it were there was plenty of oil.

Striving for perfection was doubtless a fault, Cicely supposed, arranging the forks in chevron pattern on the faded red tablecloth. She was well aware that the kinds of disasters that commonly beset her were more endearing than otherwise. Who but she would be sprayed by a skunk in her own yard while wearing a brand-new skirt? Who but she would quietly tip her station wagon over a five-foot bank while calling good night to the teacher whom she had sedately driven home from P.T.A.? In such situations there was nothing to do but laugh. She had even been able to laugh when her house burned down in Arizona, for how else could you greet the brisk consumption of all your belongings, including a new wing just completed for the children that same week? Also it had sent her to Vermont to live.

Still, she could always hope, and perhaps the only flaw in

the evening would be the almost inevitable clash between Geoffrey Toussaint and Clifton Carroll, both powerful personalities and accustomed to getting and holding the floor at any gathering. Cicely had to admit that she rather looked forward to the fireworks. She was betting on Geoffrey, who was rather more ruthless than Clifton, though no more entertaining.

One merit in being always slightly behind schedule, Cicely found, was that you never had to endure for long that fateful pause when you know everyone has forgotten the date, the time, the place, the whole occasion. The only time she had been utterly deserted by her guests was on Christmas Eve last year, when an icestorm had so glazed the roads that not even the Hiltons, always valiant, had dared to venture out. In defiance of fate and the elements Cicely had packed punch, fruit cake, cookies in a basket, and with the children shrieking and sliding with excitement had walked to the Teasdales' for one of the happiest parties of any Christmas.

Whatever pitfall was being digged for her this gentle May evening, lack of guests was not one of them. As she heard the purr of the Hiltons' station wagon she forgot her star-crossed past and, running first to light the fire, she opened the door to find that not only the Hiltons were coming up the steps, but behind them the Davenports and the Holts, always prompt.

Cicely always enjoyed her own parties as much, or possibly even more, than anyone present, especially this unacknowledged celebration of her birthday. For the guests, too, this first party of the season had a special interest, for the summer people coming up for weekend inspection of cottages and houses, and the all-year-round people putting on spring clothes for the first time, all had winter's tales to tell each other, plans to outline and absent characters to blacken or brighten according to their humor.

The last of the veal had been polished from the platter, the salad bowl was empty save for a little pool of dressing in the bottom, the mocha torte had vanished to the last crumb of meringue — Cicely as usual refusing to impart its secret — before Geoffrey Toussaint and Clifton Carroll entered the conversational lists. The long living room held small groups of Cicely's friends — Fair and Eleanor Davenport's flashing kingfisher gaze caught her eye in one corner; Wallace and Prue Holt's bright brown glance in another. Molly Hilton was asking Morris Houston about the theatrical season just past. All round the room there was the steady hum of a successful party.

Little by little, however, small groups formed larger ones until at one end of the room half the gathering listened to Clifton's stories of the modern robber baron for whom he was chief counsel, while at the other Geoffrey was spinning tales of his South Carolina youth, of fallen grandeur, seedy plantations, patronesses of the arts who did all their own work. Somehow keeping an ear on each half of the party, Cicely hoped that bringing Geoffrey and Clifton together would not result in either being vanquished on his chosen field. However, the party remained exactly divided and equally rapt, and diversion came while the battle was still equally joined.

Myrtle, the ancestral black cat of the household, just then stalked through the living room with a small limp object in her mouth, making for Cicely's downstairs bedroom. She went in and immediately came out again, returned to the kitchen and soon was back with another kitten, damp and obviously newborn. At first, in the shadowy, firelit room, her goings and comings were not much noticed, but after the third trip Eleanor Davenport, who like Cicely was partial to matriarchal cats, caught her eye and began to count softly.

Cicely sat still, trying to think where Myrtle could be taking the kittens — which spot in the clothescloset, which bureau drawer — and, more important, where she was getting them. *Four, five, six* — Myrtle seldom had more than four kittens, occasionally five — *seven, eight*; by now all conversation had lapsed and all tension vanished. As Myrtle appeared with the ninth kitten, Cicely pulled herself together and went to the kitchen. How could she have forgotten that the evening might well include diversion by the animal kingdom?

The comfortable carton she had suggested to Myrtle only yesterday sat untenanted and tidy behind the stove. Had she had them among the pots and pans again? No, all the cupboard doors were shut, for a wonder. There was the washer — but that was silly; heavens, of course, the drier! What could be more suitable — warm, dark, quiet, except, of course, when it was whirling rapidly with its light on! She peered in the open door and saw — not Myrtle's black sleekness but the arrogant green eyes and leonine ruff of Myrtle's daughter Penny. Lying with her on the pile of freshly dried, still-warm clothes were the last kittens of the two batches that had been born during and after dinner, eleven in all. Perhaps Myrtle had realized that the drier was only a temporary shelter. In any case, she had got the kittens so thoroughly mixed up that no one could ever decide which were hers and which Penny's, especially as both mothers nursed the whole lot of them in relays, one of them always on the job.

Cicely did not mind in the least sharing her bed with two cats and eleven kittens that night. After all, she owed them something for saving her party from breaking up into two armed camps. What a popular birthday mine is, she thought as she sank into contented sleep.

Menu for a Birthday Dinner

Hot Spiced Tomato Juice with Rose Hips *
Mrs. Appleyard's Cheese Biscuits †
Veal with Prosciutto *
Green Peppers Wellfleet *
Avocado, Grapefruit, Orange and Watercress Salad
Mocha Torte *
Coffee

Hot Spiced Tomato Juice with Rose Hips

Any good brand of tomato juice can be used for this. Cicely likes the Co-op brand particularly. She adds a slice or two of lemon stuck with a few cloves and a stick of cinnamon. Salt, pepper and a dash of soy sauce and garlic salt can also be used if Mrs. Appleyard is not coming. Cicely made a purée of rose hips from her ordinary garden roses when the fruits were plump and bright orange. They are said to have fifty times the vitamin C of oranges. She simmered the pulp with half a lemon for each cup of cut-up rose hips, put it through the Foley food mill and into hot sterile jars. She has to confess that it added nothing perceptible to the tomato juice except the virtuous glow of knowing so much health was there. The tomato and rose hip mixture should not be allowed to boil. Serve hot in cups, with cheese biscuits, small size, on the side.

Veal with Prosciutto

Buy enough veal, cut thin for cutlets, so that there will be one third of a pound per person. Dredge with flour, seasoned to taste, and pound with a wooden mallet till very thin. Cut in squares about four inches each way. Cut prosciutto squares the same shape. With a big French knife chop fine some thin lemon peel, garlic and parsley, also a little fresh basil if you can get it, otherwise a pinch of the dried will do. Blend the whole into a paste and smear on the squares. Add salt, pepper and a dash of cayenne and sprinkle with grated Parmigiano cheese. Put the prosciutto on top of the veal like a sandwich, roll and fasten with toothpicks. Brown the rolls in butter and set on one side. In the same frying pan — Cicely hopes you have a heavy cast-iron one — sauté some chopped green onion, a couple of capers and a cup of chopped mushrooms. Add a cup of stock and simmer for a few minutes. Stir in a teaspoonful of flour. Return the rolls to the sauce and add half a cup of white wine. Cover and cook slowly till the sauce is well blended and the rolls heated through.

Green Peppers Wellfleet

Take firm green peppers and remove the skins. Cicely puts them in a very hot oven for about ten minutes, after which it is possible to peel them. Others plunge them into boiling water or hold them over a hot flame. Either way it is a messy job and the whole process should be done at least twenty-four hours before you plan to serve your dinner. Once having got the skins off, slice the peppers lengthwise, about one half inch wide. Prepare a simple French dressing with olive oil, wine vinegar and two or three cloves of garlic. Cover the peppers with this and set them aside to absorb the flavor and the dressing. The slices will be limp and delicious.

Mocha Torte

First you must make the meringue layers for the Torte. Separate 3 eggs and beat the whites very stiff, slowly adding 1 cup sugar and 1 teaspoon almond extract. Line buttered layer cake pans with brown paper. This will make three 8-inch layers. Bake in a slow (250°) oven till done; that is, firm and a pale light brown. Cool before removing the paper.

For the filling, melt 1 package chocolate bits over hot water. Add 6 egg yolks, ¼ cup water, 2 tablespoons instant coffee, ¼ cup sugar. Blend well and cool. Beat in ⅓ pound very soft butter. To put the Torte together, spread each meringue layer with the filling and then with whipped cream. Pile them on each other and finish with whipped cream. Garnish with shavings of bitter chocolate.

Pie Plant

Spring in Vermont brings new and sometimes curious items to local menus. Long before greens of the domesticated sort are up in the gardens, wild greens are sought out, cooked and eaten. Some swear by dandelions, for salads and for cooked greens; the bitter taste must mean they are good for you, and besides, the fewer the dandelions in the lawns and fields the better. Everyone knows this except the dandelions, which continue to multiply, golden and serene, until whole fields are orange-yellow, carpeted with sunshine.

Marsh marigolds — called cowslips — outline old watercourses with their lacquered golden shine. Some cook the stems and young leaves, or toss a few of the petals in an early salad. Fiddleheads — the unfolded leaves of certain ferns — are much fancied by connoisseurs. They are said to taste like asparagus. Cicely and Mrs. Appleyard incline to prefer the real thing. On the same grounds they would rather have lobster than rattlesnake meat.

The Appleyard ladies make dandelion and cowslip wine, in an attempt to bottle the first spring sunshine for winter consumption. But for true eating pleasure they watch for the first upthrust of rhubarb through last year's tangled grass. A rhubarb plant, like horseradish, is almost eternal, and no matter how much you cut it, it still greets the spring with unimpaired zeal.

True to their principle of eating everything in season, Cicely and her mother, the latter in town briefly to see that her house is still standing after the winter, keep large bowls of stewed rhubarb on hand in the refrigerator. Patience Barlow constructs latticed rhubarb pie. Rhubarb baked with sliced oranges adorns the luncheon table. Vanilla ice cream displays a rhubarb sauce. The wry astringent flavor of pie plant can be met during every course of the meal on certain over-enthusiastic days. It deters Mrs. Appleyard and her daughter not at all that the rest of the members of their family do not share their passion for rhubarb. All the more for them.

The ancestral Appleyard rhubarb plants are of a medium red strain that produces a beautiful pink sauce. As long as they pick only the fresh young stalks the sauce will be neither bitter nor stringy. Part of the pleasure in the rhubarb season is in the picking. Cicely's plants are down beside the brook, so that as she fills her basket she can inspect the water level, check on the wild flowers in the ravine where she planted them last year and see whether the bluebird has taken advantage of the hollow in the apple tree for this year's nest.

As Mrs. Appleyard pulls her stalks of rhubarb beside her back steps, the barn swallows swoop over her head and across her man-made pond in the pasture, now blending into the landscape. She sees that the frost has as usual pulled the carriage house about and that the barn floor lists still further to the south than it did. Somehow all Vermont buildings are trying to get to Florida. One more limb has gone from her bird tree. Soon it will be fit for nothing but a pecking post for pileated woodpeckers.

As the rhubarb season blends into the strawberry season, Mrs. Appleyard and Cicely make preserves combining both these favorites of theirs. This too is a good sauce for ice cream or on a plain cake. They halfheartedly freeze a little rhubarb, but their passion for it is waning. They toy with the idea of rhubarb ice cream and postpone it till next year. As the tones of the new leaves lose their distinction and blend more and more into a uniform green, as the orchard grass grows long and hides the rhubarb plants, these ladies occupy themselves more and more with their gardens. Rhubarb is part of the wild open look of early spring, not sedate enough for summer when the greens march in neat rows across the tamed earth.

Supper Menu in Rhubarb Time

Smothered Chicken *
Cream of Wheat Spoon Bread
Spinach Ring * with Mushroom Sauce (p. 116)
Rhubarb and Strawberry Conserve *
Hot Mocha Chocolate
Rhubarb Ice Cream
    or
Latticed Rhubarb Pie with Vanilla Ice Cream
    or
Baked Rhubarb and Orange Slices *

Smothered Chicken (V. H.)

Have a broiling chicken weighing at least 2½ pounds cut into four pieces. Use the wing tips, neck and carefully scrubbed and manicured (or is it pedicured?) feet to make a broth with onion, celery, carrot and whatever seasonings you like. While this is simmering you may do whatever you wish for a couple of hours. Mrs. Appleyard enjoys a good game of chess but does not consider it necessary to impose this preference upon the general public. About an hour and a half before serving time put some seasoned flour into a paper bag and toss the pieces of chicken around in it until they are thoroughly coated. Then brown them carefully in a mixture of half butter and half lard over a rather low flame, turning them from time to time. Use a heavy iron frying pan. They should be an even golden brown. Now strain in about two cups of the broth. Turn the heat down as low as it will go and simmer the chicken until it is tender, about an hour and a quarter. Add a little broth occasionally. There will be a delicious light brown gravy in the pan when the chicken is done. The small pieces of meat, the vegetables and the rest of the broth can be used in a risotto another day.

Variation (Mrs. Appleyard): Make your broth with tomato juice instead of water. Add to the chicken green pepper, sliced onions, mushrooms sautéed in butter just before you pour the broth over it. Add chopped parsley when you serve it.

Variation No. 2: Make your broth with water. Add sautéed mushrooms and onions when you pour the broth over the chicken. Just before serving time, remove the chicken from the pan. Blend in a little white wine, about two tablespoons, and half a cup of sour cream. Let it heat but not boil or it will curdle. Sprinkle a few minced chives or some minced parsley over it.

Spinach Ring

One of the few things that is better out of a cellophane bag than it is from your own garden, Mrs. Appleyard says, is spinach. Somehow no amateur ever gets the sand out of spinach so well as the people who wash it professionally. Perhaps they have a kind of super-Bendix that whirls it clean. Prue Holt tried it in her washing machine, and the problem was not so much how to get sand out of the spinach as how to get spinach out of Wallace's shirts for the next few weeks. Anyway, there it is, clean, curled and green. Your only problem is to get rid of the bag.

"I saw in the paper that you can use cellophane for mulch in the vegetable garden," Mrs. Appleyard remarked to Venetia Hopkins.

Venetia is the kind of gardener who will herself distribute a ton of straw between her rows of lettuce and peas. She grows delphinium eight feet high and lilies the size of Gabriel's trumpet. There is a story, circulated by some rival lover of compost, no doubt, that a weed was once seen in her asparagus bed.

Mrs. Appleyard doesn't believe a word of it.

"You save the cellophane and use it from year to year," she added.

Venetia made the noise usually written "Humph," and Mrs. Appleyard put the cellophane in the stove, touched a match to it and went to work as follows:

For a ring mold that would serve six people she took:

2 bags of washed spinach	¼ cup water
1 tablespoon finely minced onion	4 eggs, not separated
1 cup milk, part cream	3 tablespoons flour
3 tablespoons butter	¼ teaspoon nutmeg
4 slices Pepperidge Farm bread	¼ teaspoon pepper
	salt to taste

Make croutons from 4 slices of Pepperidge Farm bread and brown them slowly and lightly in 2 extra tablespoons of butter. Toss them frequently. Use garlic butter if you like it and are sure your guests will.

Cook the spinach and onion in the water until the spinach is thoroughly wet and limp, turning it over frequently. This takes about 4 minutes. Put ⅓ cup of the milk and water from the spinach in the electric blender. Add half the spinach and purée it thoroughly, then the rest in two more lots. Or use your own purée method. A food mill is a good tool for this. Or chop it and run it through the finest blade of the meat chopper. Anyway, get it fine and it should be cooked so little that it is still bright green. Light the oven at 325° and put a pan of hot water on the lower shelf.

Melt the butter, add flour and seasonings slowly and rub the mixture smooth. Remove from heat and slowly stir in the remaining ¾ cup of milk. Cook over a low flame till it thickens. Stir in the spinach purée. Mix in the eggs, one at a time, beating after each addition. Give it a final beating, pour it into a well-buttered ring mold, set it in the oven and bake until a knife blade dipped into it comes out clean — about 35 minutes. Run a spatula around the outer edge, a small knife around the inner one. Invert the mold on a circular dish.

Fill with Mushroom Sauce (p. 116). Surround with the croutons.

Baked Rhubarb and Orange Slices

To 4 cups rhubarb washed and cut in inch-long pieces add 4 oranges, peeled and cut in slices, 2 cups of sugar and a twist of lemon rind. Fill an earthenware baking dish with alternate layers of rhubarb and oranges, sprinkling with sugar in between. Bury the lemon peel in the middle. Bake in a fairly hot oven — 375° — till it bubbles around the edges. Serve with hard sauce. This also makes a good filling for a deep dish rhubarb pie.

Rhubarb and Strawberry Conserve

In any standard recipe for jam, take equal parts rhubarb and strawberries and follow the usual procedure. This makes a good ice-cream sauce.

Birthday Picnic

THE APPLEYARD FAMILY has many picnic sites. There is Jump-on-Appletree Pasture, where the stunted trees have been nibbled down by generations of cows till their twigs are like iron, capable of supporting a middle-sized child. There is Where-Grandma-Spilled-the-Lemonade-and-Was-Cross — a cow pasture halfway up Spruce Mountain referred to in awed terms by Mrs. Appleyard's children; their mother has often mislaid things, but seldom her temper.

Over toward Catamount is the pasture where the Bradshaws and the Hiltons were dining *al fresco* together when they found the first wild mushrooms. In the other direction is an overgrown cellar hole on a hillcrest overlooking Millbrook Pond. A birch tree and a maple have grown up in the cellar hole and the Appleyards sit on the wide granite doorstep and watch the wind send catspaws over the pond.

However, for the picnic with which Mrs. Appleyard and Camilla, the youngest Bradshaw, celebrate their joint birthday, the family almost always decides on Stone Houses for their picnic spot. Just at the edge of the spruce woods that border the Appleyard sugarbush is a series of ledges. The slates have

been used to make a fireplace and two thronelike chairs for
the guests of honor. One of them was always haunted for
Cicely by the shade of her Grandmother Appleyard, energetic,
salty of tongue, earthy of wit. Cicely remembered her playing
billiards in her petticoat during a thunderstorm, going out to the
garden at midnight to peel and eat a cucumber, sending her a
check for a thousand dollars as a graduation present, to do with
as she pleased.

The view from the picnic seats spread the whole of Appleyard Center before them like a toy village. They could see
Henry Gould drive the last of his sleek brown Jerseys into
the barn for milking and Marcia shutting up the hens for the
night. Frank Flint drove his yellow mail car down the hill,
pausing at each box to slide the papers and letters in with the
deftness of long practice. They watched in turn the Goulds,
the Marshes, the Balches come out to get their mail. In the
still clear air of late afternoon every sound rose to them un-
diluted, and they could hear Sandra Marsh call to her husband and see him come out on the porch.

"There must be a letter from Jim," said Mrs. Appleyard.
"I do hope it's good news." She knew from her own long
years of waiting for letters from Stan and Hugh while they
were in the service how hard it was to be calm when any series
of letters was interrupted.

Tommy Bradshaw was building a fire and fitting the grate
over it for Hamburg Specials. Cicely laid out brown bowls
of fixings — sliced tomatoes, green pepper rings, mild onion
slices, lengths of sharp cheese from the creamery over the
ridge, last year's chutney and red pepper relish. Cynthia
Bradshaw, formerly nicknamed Moppet, toasted the hamburger
rolls to order. Joan handed out wooden plates and paper nap-

kins. Camilla prepared to circulate with the salt grinder and pepper grater. She was too giddy with birthday excitement to sit still on her throne.

Mrs. Appleyard, however, was content to look about her and be waited upon. What did it matter if the hamburgers were a little charred on the outside, a little raw within, the rolls unevenly toasted, more pepper on her skirt than on her meat? Lately her birthdays had drifted by her with increasing frequency, but she could still share the intensity of Camilla's anticipation of the joys of being five.

Hamburgers having been devoured, Cicely retired into the spruce trees and came out with the birthday cake lit with six candles.

"I knew you wouldn't object to having Camilla dictate the number of candles," she said to her mother.

"Certainly not," said Mrs. Appleyard. "I don't care to have my cake bristling like a porcupine."

"You came to see me in the hospital, Grandma," said Camilla suddenly. "I was as big as a cat and I had black eyes."

"So you did, and black hair too," said her grandmother. "I liked you right away. Here, blow out the candles and I'll cut the cake."

With a great puff Camilla blew out all the candles. Cicely removed the daffodils from the center of the cake, her mother cut it in generous pieces and in no time at all there was nothing left but a smear of yellow frosting and a few crumbs. Angel cakes were a tradition for Appleyard birthdays, trimmed with flowers of the appropriate season, frosted and colored according to individual taste. Hugh always used to have pussy willows on his, Cicely pansies, Sally lilacs and Stan roses. But that was in Massachusetts, and Vermont birthdays for the same people had different flowers. Thus Mrs. Appleyard who in Brookline shared lilacs with Sally, in Appleyard Center was put back to daffodils.

By the time the picnic odds and ends had been burned, the sun was heading for the gap between Catamount and Hunger Mountain and the shadows were creeping up the fields toward Stone Houses. Joan and Camilla were called away from a building project on the lower ledge where generations of Appleyards had made Druid circles, villages of cones and twigs, quartz pebbles, twisted roots. Tommy had collected enough spruce gum to last about a week.

Cynthia's sharp eyes saw the car turn in to her grandmother's yard before the rest had noticed anything. It was a long, low-slung black convertible with the top down. Since the passengers had alighted and were standing on the porch, the scarlet leather upholstery was brilliantly visible.

"Ah," said Mrs. Appleyard, "I expect I am wanted below." She meant, of course, that she hoped she was wanted.

Who doesn't?

"We're just going anyway," said Cicely. "Give your grandmother a hand, Tommy — no, not the one with the spruce gum in it. Is it the Emperor Geoffrey Toussaint the First?"

"None other," replied her mother joyfully. "Probably he wishes to consult me about some satin-backed wallpaper or a marble dressing table. I heard that he was to be in residence today."

Now, she thought, things would begin to hum around Appleyard Center. One composer would start to play Bach on that piano that sounds like a banjo when you put down the middle pedal while another was trying over his new twelve-tone piece on the Steinway. Painters would begin painting their friends with four eyes, all crossed. Writers would hide their tape recorders in their hosts' living rooms and transcribe the tapes with pens dipped in a nice blend of maple syrup and vitriol.

"Come on, children," she said aloud. "Summer's begun!"

Menu for a Birthday Picnic

Hamburg Specials *
Red Pepper Relish †
Apple Chutney (p. 103)
Angel Cake with Flowers of the Season *

Mrs. Appleyard lived so long before the invention of electric grinders that it was many years before she knew there was such a thing as Hamburg steak. In her innocent youth tough steak was pounded, and usually not enough. On the whole, in case any archaeologist of the future would like to know, she considers the Ground Meat era superior to the Pounded Meat period. She would like, however, to record the fact that, like a freezer, you can't really get better meat out of a grinder than you put into it. Tenderer, yes, but not better flavored or with a better proportion of lean to fat meat. She thinks it is worthwhile to pay more and have chuck or bottom of the round ground — twice — for you. She also asserts that hamburgers ought to be big enough, at least a third of a pound apiece, and that one large one is better than two small ones.

The length of time they are cooked will be a matter of taste. She likes them brown on the outside, pink — not raw —

inside and achieves this effect by doing them two minutes on each side in a heated iron frying pan. In getting them ready she mixes about a tablespoonful of cold water with a pound of ground lean meat, shapes and pats each cake firmly, and conceals a small lump of butter, half a teaspoonful, in the center of each.

With sliced young onions from the garden, rich red tomato slices still warm from the vines, her own piccalilli and chutney, mustard pickle and horseradish with sour cream, she considers the eating of hamburgers no penance. She just wishes the rolls were not made out of cotton. She knows that the production of cotton is one of our major industries but she thinks it ought to be used for the lining of comforters. Perhaps, she says generously, it would be better with caraway seeds in it. At least it would be a good place to put them. Mrs. Appleyard was charmed, on a brief visit to Mexico, to learn that the importation of caraway seeds into that country is prohibited.

She ate one of the best meals she ever had in her life in a cave dug out of a brown hill in Mexico. Inside, the cave was painted a sinister neon blue. No caraway seeds in anything. No hamburgers either. Juicy steak, two inches thick. *Viva Mexico!*

Returning to everyday life, Mrs. Appleyard recalls with pleasure a way Venetia Hopkins has of treating Hamburg steak.

Hamburg Pie

For four people use an 8-inch frying pan and 1¾ pounds of ground meat. Butter the pan lightly, put the meat in, all in one thick cake pressed down evenly. Cook it for 5 minutes on top of the stove over a hot flame, then for 4 minutes under a preheated gas broiler or radiant electric broiler. This produces a medium-rare effect. Increase both times slightly if you like it better done.

To go with it, in a separate frying pan, she makes either a tomato sauce with garlic and green pepper (p. 53) or a mushroom sauce (p. 116), pouring it, bubbling hot, over the Hamburg Pie just before she brings it to the table.

Variation: Hamburg Pie Pretty Nearly Stroganov

Who was Stroganov? No one has been able to answer this question for Mrs. Appleyard. All anyone replies is "Well, you take some sour cream . . . " Mrs. Appleyard took a cupful, but first she began by slicing three onions thin and cooking them in butter until they began to brown. Then she poured 2 cups of hot water over them and turned the heat down. When she next looked at them all the water was cooked out and the onions were a deep amber color. She then proceeded to cook the Hamburg Pie as above (1¾ pounds of ground steak in an 8-inch buttered frying pan, 5 minutes on top of the stove, 4 minutes under the electric broiler). In the meantime she stirred the sour cream into the onions and let it stand, unheated. Just before the Hamburg was ready she heated the mixture to the boiling point, then poured it around the edge where the "pie" had shrunk from the pan, sprinkled it with parsley on top, and served it in the pan. The Hamburg cooked this way was juicy enough so that juice ran into the onion and sour cream mixture.

"Very good," pronounced Hugh Appleyard who was greeted with this invention at the end of a thousand-mile drive. "Well worth coming for."

He also enjoyed kasha, and peas twenty minutes from the vines. They drank Stroganov's health, whoever he was, in a glass of Burgundy.

Angel Cake

Mrs. Appleyard has made a good many angel cakes in her career in which she actually dealt with 13 egg whites and later with 13 yolks. She tells how she used to do this in *Mrs. Appleyard's Kitchen* (p. 56). That, however, was not a summer kitchen. It was quite a while before Cicely and her mother admitted to each other that their fine old New England moral fiber had relaxed so that they were using packaged angel cake mix. In fact they probably never would have admitted it to each other if they had not happened to meet at the counter in the Co-op, Cicely with a package of Swansdown, and her mother with one of Pillsbury's. Each maintains staunchly that her own brand is the best. The public — and this is definitely embarrassing — doesn't seem to be able to tell the difference either between one package and another or between a package and the 13-egg masterpieces of Auld Lang Syne. Mrs. Appleyard's advice is to choose whatever kind attracts you and to follow the directions *exactly*.

Menu for a Supper in May

Fried Chicken
Wild Rice with Sautéed Mushrooms
Asparagus with Horse-radish and Sour Cream (p. 62)

Tossed Fruit and Scallion Salad *
Orange Cake *
Coffee

When Mrs. Appleyard was opening her house for what in
Vermont is quaintly called the summer — a season consisting
of a warm weekend in late July — it was May. Hills were
freshly frosted with snow. She had lunched on a lettuce sandwich. Of course the day was beautiful. Spring peepers were
tinkling. Meadows looked up at the blue sky out of bluer pools
of melted ice. Gray poplars were hung with silver catkins.
Brooks ran fast and green, foaming white over hidden rocks.
Under the golden willows rivers brimmed their banks.

Still, Mrs. Appleyard cannot live entirely on the landscape
and she was delighted when Laura Parkes asked her to supper.
Laura claims she is not a bit interested in food, hates to cook
and the meal would be terrible. Mrs. Appleyard knew that
Laura, though originally from Massachusetts, had lived in her
big white house in Montpelier long enough to have picked up
some Vermont attitudes. She did not worry about supper.
Mrs. Parkes might not be interested in what she ate herself
but she was far from indifferent to the appetites of her guests.

It was no surprise, therefore, when Laura bade her guest sit
down and listen to E. Power Biggs playing a Bach fugue on
an ancient Dutch organ and then, apparently without lifting
a finger, produced the above menu. Her generosity did not
stop there. After the meal was over she read to Mrs. Appleyard out of her own hand-written cookbook, read slowly
enough so Mrs. Appleyard could write it all down and pass
it along.

Tossed Fruit and Scallion Salad

sections from 1 grapefruit and   1 green pepper, sliced thin
   1 orange   1 bunch scallions, finely cut
1 avocado, diced   lettuce

Toss all together with your favorite French dressing.

Orange Cake

Grind together:

1 cup raisins   rind of 1 orange
1 cup walnuts

In the mixer cream ½ cup butter with 1 cup sugar.
Beat in 2 eggs.

                      1 cup sour milk or ¾ cup
2 cups flour sifted with 1 tea-   sweet milk and ¼ cup malt
   spoon soda   vinegar

Combine mixtures. Bake at 325° until the top springs back
when pressed with the finger and the cake shrinks from the
side of the pan — about 40 minutes. Remove from the pan
and while the cake is still hot pour over it the juice of a large
orange in which has been thoroughly dissolved ¾ cup sugar.
This cake keeps well and is the kind of thing to give you
courage to face the spring. Mrs. Appleyard was given a large
chunk of it and found it extremely nutritious.

June

The Garden is Green

When Mrs. Appleyard drives into her yard in June the first thing she notices is the way it smells. The spice pinks are out in a scented pink ruff around the bed of hardy perennials. These are well-named plants as only the hardiest can survive Mrs. Appleyard's patronage, which somehow produces more grass than flowers. Syringas, however, continue to send out perfume in response to her affectionate neglect. White rugosa roses positively revel in it. Pekin lilac demands no care to produce a fountain of creamy white, sweet-smelling spray.

Roger Willard has cut the grass, and in the fields across the

brook tall timothy with clover in it is freshly mown. To shut
off your engine and put your head out the car window is like
opening the lid of an enormous jar of pot-pourri.

It is not possible to live entirely on pot-pourri, as Mrs.
Appleyard soon remembers. It takes only a little longer to
realize that in Appleyard Center she must drop back into a
sort of neolithic age in which the procuring of each item of
food is a personal triumph for the hunter. The weapons are
different it is true. Little can be accomplished with bow
and arrow; much with a wide-ranging car, a keen eye and
a persuasive tongue.

Perhaps it is only because she drives forty miles to get it,
but Vermont asparagus seems to have a distinctive flavor. She
learned long ago from Mr. Appleyard to eat whatever is in
season every day while it is at its best; that when the season
is over something else comes along. So she eats asparagus:
country style, with Hollandaise, as soup, as shortcake with
cream sauce, cold with French dressing, hot with garlic croutons. By the time asparagus is getting stringy there are radishes
and lettuce, five kinds of it, in her own garden, and the purple
flowers of chives are coming up among the spice pinks.

It is obviously time to make spring garden salad and invite
some guests who like garlic. She will serve Mr. Appleyard's
Welsh Rabbit too. She will not buy any English muffins
constructed with a view to using as much air and as little flour
as possible. She states that she will make crumpets herself
for the Welsh Rabbit to cascade over.

There is plenty of the 1955 chutney in the cellarway and
it was a fairly good vintage, she remembers, and likely to
have mellowed with age. Strawberries will be in season so
soon that those left in the freezer from last year had better

be used, she tells Patience Barlow. Perhaps for sauce on some angel cake. Patience gets out her egg beater and suggests that some guests with good digestions had better be chosen.

"And what," she asks with a slight touch of severity, "are you going to do with thirteen egg yolks?"

She should not have challenged Mrs. Appleyard's ingenuity. That lady stops mixing her crumpets long enough to assert that fish mousse with plenty of Hollandaise sauce, and crème brûlée will take care of most of them. Cicely suggests a gold cake that will cope with the rest.

"I'll invite some people who are on a bland diet for that menu," Mrs. Appleyard adds, and names over a few of her friends who have ulcers, or, as she has heard them called, dental difficulties. "I'll ask the ones with gallstones another day," she adds considerately.

"Well, don't serve spoon bread the same time you do fish mousse," Patience Barlow advises.

She is referring to one of Mrs. Appleyard's less well-planned luncheons during which a nearsighted guest put maple syrup on the fish mousse and Hollandaise on the spoon bread.

"I always knew Vermonters served a great deal of maple syrup but not with fish," the lady is reported to have said with an air of bewilderment.

Mrs. Appleyard simply remarked cheerfully that it was fortunate that no one had put hard sauce on the green beans or horseradish with sour cream on the chocolate soufflé. (Both were available.) She then set her crumpet batter to rise and did a little work on her velvet painting. June — that charming chilly month — usually brings out her latent handcraftiness. This year it is taking the form of trying to paint on velvet as well as her great-grandmother did a hundred and thirty years ago. So far her great-grandmother is still ahead. As she combines grapes and peaches and plums in a blue bowl, Mrs. Appleyard admires her ancestress more and more.

"Of course hers has had time to mellow," she says. "But I'll soon fix that."

As a gentle beauty hint one of Mrs. Appleyard's descendants once presented her with some pancake make-up. Mrs. Appleyard tried it but soon concluded that she looked too much like a beech leaf left over from last autumn and stopped using it. Naturally, being a Vermonter if only by association, she did not throw it away. It proved to be just the thing for mellowing velvet paintings. Mrs. Appleyard has plenty on hand in case a similar problem arises.

LUNCHEON MENUS

Mr. Appleyard's Welsh Rabbit † with English muffins
       or
Cheese Fondue with Toasted French Bread
Asparagus, Country Style
Absent-Minded Meringue,* Crushed Strawberries
Tea

Fish Mousse with Hollandaise †
Asparagus with Garlic Croutons
Inside out Potatoes *
Tossed Salad
Crème Brûlée *
Coffee

Iced Vichyssoise

Rock Cornish Chickens *
Corn Pudding †
Asparagus Vinaigrette *
No Dessert except Soufflé Crackers † and Cheese

Absent-Minded Meringue

5 egg whites
1 teaspoon cream of tartar

1½ cups sugar
1 teaspoon vanilla

Beat the egg whites till they begin to thicken. Sprinkle in the cream of tartar and beat them until they are thick. Beat in half the sugar, a little at a time; fold in the rest and the vanilla. Put the mixture into an 8-inch aluminum pan lined with brown paper and bake it at 350° for half an hour. Turn off the oven. Forget the meringue and leave it in the oven all night.

You will have to arrange your own system for overlooking this delicacy. Mrs. Appleyard did it by being called to the telephone for a long distance talk with one of her favorite characters (note: Long distance in this case refers to the time consumed in conversation, not to the physical distance which is 1¼ miles) and prudently turning off the oven, planning to turn it on again later. Luckily she forgot and began to read *Wuthering Heights* for the seventeenth time. In the morning the meringue was a delicately tinted square of crispness which she split, filled with ice cream, and served with fresh raspberries.

Meringues

5 egg whites

1 cup granulated sugar, sifted
1 teaspoon vanilla

In case you are in a mood to pay attention to the baking of meringues, Mrs. Appleyard, who has produced her share of flabby and sticky ones in her time, gives the following baking suggestions.

Beat egg whites in a cold bowl until they are thick but not stiff. Light the oven: 275°. Add sugar a tablespoon at a time, beating well, until you have used ¾ of a cup. Fold in the remaining ¼ cup of sugar and the vanilla. Cover a cooky sheet with a double thickness of white typewriter paper. (This is Mrs. Appleyard's favorite use for this substance. She always uses the best grade. The ordinary kind is plenty good enough for writing per cent signs when she means — well, what? Better not be too precise.) Spoon on the mixture in circular heaps. This amount makes ten large ones. Bake them until there are no shiny bubbles on them. *None. Not any.* It will take at least an hour. If your oven does not bake evenly, turn the pan. Be careful to do it gently and as quickly as possible so that the cold air does not strike them for any length of time. Mrs. Appleyard speaks, if at all, while shifting the pan in much the same low voice that she uses when she is shown her newest grandchild. She says meringues, like her descendants, behave best when the barometer is rising. Remove them immediately from the paper. Store them until you use them in a tin box with a tight-fitting lid.

Inside out Potatoes

Scrub large symmetrical potatoes, allowing one to a person and one or two extra. They need not be Idahos but they should be oval in shape and without bumps. Allow an hour and five minutes from sink to plate. Have the oven preheated at 450°.

Bake the potatoes at this temperature for twenty minutes, turning them often the first 10 minutes. Reduce the heat to 350°, turn them again and bake thirty minutes longer. Take them out of the oven, split them carefully lengthwise, remove the contents to a warm bowl containing softened butter, salt and freshly ground pepper to taste, and a little thick cream stirred together. Mash the potatoes briskly into the butter and cream. A large fork with twisted blades or a sturdy spoon with holes in it will help you at this point. Heap the mixture into the shells, set them in a pan and run it under the broiler briefly until a golden brown color appears.

Variations: Chopped chives or parsley may be stirred into the mixture.

It may be topped with thinly sliced Cheddar cheese.

Bacon cooked on one side, drained, and cut into small pieces may be put on top, cooked side down.

Crème Brûlée

8 egg yolks	1 quart light cream
2 tablespoons sugar	2 teaspoons vanilla
1 cup (about) light brown sugar	

You must have dry light brown sugar. The package will be labeled yellow brown or golden brown. Dark brown *will not do.*

You will need a cup, possibly more. The amount will vary with the size of the dish you use. Mrs. Appleyard likes a 9 x 13 Pyrex one. This gives plenty of top in proportion to the depth.

Heat the cream but do not scald it. Add sugar and vanilla

and pour the mixture over the well-beaten egg yolks and then into the Pyrex dish. Set the dish into a pan of warm water and bake it at 350° until a silver knife slipped into the middle comes out clean (about 20 minutes). Chill the custard — that's what it is, we may as well face it — for several hours or overnight. When it is very cold, cover it ¼ inch deep with the light brown sugar which is well sifted and free from lumps.

Now the broiling: an electric infra-red broiler is fine but it can be done in a gas broiler. Light either one ahead of time: gas, 5 minutes, electric infra-red 1 minute. The idea is brief exposure to intense heat. You must watch the Brûlée every second or it will scorch. All you are trying to do is to melt the sugar as fast as possible. When it begins to brown, remove it at once from the flame.

The center usually melts first so it is a good idea to slide first one end of the pan and then the other under the flame. The whole melting process takes three minutes, perhaps less. Now chill the Brûlée again. The top should be like golden ice and when tapped with the spoon should give forth a pleasant resonance.

Rock Cornish Chickens

These come frozen, beautifully trussed, encased in plastic bags and stuffed with wild rice. There are cooking directions printed on the plastic and they are helpful, but Mrs. Appleyard naturally has a suggestion or two.

Put the birds — one apiece — into a covered roaster right in their plastic bags. Have the oven 325°–350°. After an hour remove the bags. This is not so easy as it sounds, something

like juggling a hot greased pig. After you have won the battle
— and good luck to you! — pour melted butter over the
chickens, then dredge them with flour seasoned as you like
it. You were saving, Mrs. Appleyard hopes, some chicken
fat and some broth for just such an emergency. Put the fat
into the pan. There will soon be enough liquid to baste the
birds. Do this every fifteen minutes until they are brown and
tender. This should be in about another hour. Now remove
them to a hot platter and make gravy in the roaster.

Mrs. Appleyard uses for four birds:

2 tablespoons flour   2 tablespoons onion relish (p.
2 tablespoons chopped parsley   217) or finely minced onion
1½ cups milk   1½ cups chicken broth, hot
                        salt to taste

Cook the onion till it softens. Rub flour into the fat. Cook
till it thickens and starts to brown. Turn off the heat, blend
in the stock and the milk. Add any seasoning you like, or
leave it to lead its own life. Reheat, sprinkle the parsley over
it and serve birds and gravy.

Asparagus Vinaigrette

When you have served Asparagus with Hollandaise, with
lemon butter, country style, made shortcake and used the tips
moistened with heavy cream for filling, or put piles of it with
green mayonnaise around cold boiled salmon, you might like
to change and try it vinaigrette, like this:

Break off the stalks of two and a half pounds of asparagus
where they snap easily, boil them until tender in your aspara-

gus cooker if you have one. Otherwise tie them in a neat bunch, trim off the stems so the bunch will stand up. They should cook standing for ten minutes and then covered by the boiling water for another seven to ten minutes. Do not overcook or the tips will break off.

Drain, and while the asparagus is still warm, pour over it the following sauce.

6 tablespoons olive oil	1 tablespoon tarragon vinegar
2 tablespoons Wesson oil	2 tablespoons cider vinegar
1 tablespoon minced piccalilli	1 tablespoon green pepper
1 teaspoon minced parsley	minced

1 tablespoon minced chives

Seasonings to taste: salt, 1 teaspoon paprika, pepper from the grinder, ½ teaspoon mustard.

Put these all in a jar and shake well. Put the asparagus into a serving dish lightly rubbed with garlic. Set the dish into the refrigerator. Serve it very cold. If the evening is hot, set the dish into another containing cracked ice. Garnish with grated egg yolk and strips of pimento.

Mrs. Appleyard always feels slightly abused when the subject of asparagus comes up, as it does every spring. For a long time her wistfully hungry expression expressed regret that she hadn't planted a bed of it the season before. Years passed; in fact, decades passed. At last the time, the place and the loved one all synchronized. Mary Washington was her name. Her appearance was something that only Shakespeare, George Meredith and the man who wrote the catalogue, probably assisted by Robert Browning, could properly describe. A thousand roots cost only $20.

"Was this the face that launched a thousand roots?" mur-

mured Mrs. Appleyard, writing out the check lightly though
with emotion.

So they came and were planted and the rest had better be
silence. We did just happen to hear Mrs. Appleyard announce,
one crisp May evening when everyone else within ten miles
of Appleyard Center was saying: "I wonder when the peas
will be ripe. I get kind of tired of asparagus this time of year
. . ." that at least she was the only gardener she knew whose
asparagus had cost her ten dollars a stalk.

"One of them," she added proudly, "was as large as my
fourth finger."

Luckily the neighbors are generous.

Eating up the Freezer

O NE of the interesting features of Mrs. Appleyard's return
to Vermont is seeing what she left in her drawer in the Locker
Plant the year before. There are said to be individuals who
keep accurate records of the frozen food they have on hand,
who can tell with a quick glance at a filing card how many
green beans are left and when they ate the last of that uninteresting batch of chicken soup. Not so Mrs. Appleyard. To
her everything is a glad surprise — well, a surprise anyway.

The Locker Plant is a sort of gastronomic grab bag. Some of the grabs are more popular than others. As she examines the pearls of her dietetic rosary and counts them over one by one before putting them back into her own freezer, Mrs. Appleyard makes certain resolutions.

She will not, she promises herself, freeze any more succotash. There's a two years' supply on hand now. It must have been pure nervousness in 1953 that caused her to construct all that spaghetti sauce. Why, there's still enough to take a bath in. Also she will use everything up before she puts anything more in. And she will pack everything systematically, the oldest on top.

These virtuous resolves have something hauntingly familiar about them. They last several days. Within a week she has returned to her old habits — using the creamed mushrooms and letting the succotash sink to the bottom, cooking fresh rhubarb when she ought to be eating 1952 blackberries, bringing out her own peach ice cream and letting the sherbet of the professionals keep its own granite hardness and flavor. Still, she does find a delicious pot roast she had forgotten. She discovers that some of her guests — the ones who went with her on a picnic to visit a clairvoyant, for instance — are hungry enough in the open air to eat a casserole containing *both* the spaghetti sauce and the succotash.

Everyone knows that there is something special about Vermont turkeys and maple syrup, but few realize that Vermont clairvoyants also have their peculiar excellence. There is something charmingly cosy about prophecy combined with understatement. No crystal ball, no cobwebs are needed, no mystic symbols, no dingy shawls. A Vermont clairvoyant can operate in a sunshiny room with crisp ruffled curtains at the windows.

You may find her washing dishes at her spotless sink, wearing an apron flowered like a June meadow. She helps you state your problem by offering you coffee and freshly made doughnuts.

Even Mrs. Appleyard, a natural skeptic, likes a clairvoyant who says "I guess." Certainly the episode of the Bradshaws' silver takes some explaining. Somehow it vanished at the time their house in Arizona burned down. Cicely was quite sure she had not taken it to Arizona, and yet when she came back to Vermont to live there was no trace of it. Her mother knew nothing about it. She remembered buying it at the time of Cicely's wedding, remembered the maroon bags it came in and the plain pattern like her own, her mother's and her grandmother's, but she had not seen it for years. A common characteristic of the younger generation, Mrs. Appleyard has noticed, is that, for sensible reasons to do with the vanishing of servants, they are not metal polishers. The Bradshaws eat happily with stainless steel. However, there are occasions when a dozen teaspoons and salad forks come in handy, and when one of these arose Cicely missed her silver. Always efficient, she decided, rather than to ransack the house any further, to go to Berylla Casilani's.

Berylla lives on the other side of a substantial range of hills (mountains to southerners from Massachusetts). Mrs. Appleyard decided to take anyone in the neighborhood who had a problem in the lost-and-found department and a picnic lunch. She got out her various containers for hot and cold dishes, constructed her casserole and extracted other items from the freezer, reducing its contents to a satisfactory extent.

The travelers ate their lunch on a picnic table in a mountain glen beside a noisy foaming brook. The blackflies had been planning apparently to lunch on the picnickers. How did they know lunch was coming?

"Consulted Berylla, perhaps," Mrs. Appleyard said, and produced a bottle of 612 from the basket, for like Mrs. Swiss Family Robinson she comes prepared for pretty nearly everything. Thus garnished, the party consumed the casserole in peace and ate the 1953 cinnamon buns. They drank the punch, left over from Labor Day last year. They ate the Brown Betty made from last year's applesauce. The hard sauce was contemporary, but the cheese had been aged, though not by Mrs. Appleyard.

Thus refreshed they drove on through lanes of elms hung with fresh green, along the river bottom with its serpentine steep-banked stream, past a tiny sway-backed covered bridge and so to Berylla's tidy farmhouse.

Found after conference this day were one Stillson wrench, one platinum and diamond wrist watch, one Jersey heifer and a certain amount of flat silver. Perhaps the circumstances of the finding of the watch were the most unusual. Its owner had visited Berylla to inquire about a diamond ring (it was right where she left it, on the kitchen table with a Sandwich glass salt cellar turned over it). Not long afterward she missed the watch. Berylla handed it to her as soon as she spoke about it.

"The children found it in the road," she said. "I kinda guessed the owner would turn up. You musta dropped it last time you were here. No, I won't take a cent, no charge for storage."

A clairvoyant who would not make capital of such a heaven-sent occurrence must be of a really devastating honesty, Mrs. Appleyard decided. Apparently it never occurred to her to

put the watch in a hollow tree and send the owner there blind-
folded at midnight, telling her to put her hand in the hole when
the owl hooted thrice. But then Berylla does not write mystery
stories.

She was now thinking about Cicely's silver. She rocked a
little in her old Boston rocker. She was knitting a pink baby
blanket and her needles stopped clicking for a minute as though
she were drowsy.

"Well," she said gently, "I guess your silver didn't burn
up in any fire. I don't know as it's in Vermont, though. Seems
'sif I see it in some other state south of here. It's in a kind of
a big house, a white house up a ways from the street, quite a
few steps. It's not a country place, but there's a lot of grass
and trees. The silver's quite high up in the house, about as
high as you can get. I guess ther's something near it that's
dark red . . . I'm afraid it's not much help," she added apolo-
getically, "but you're entitled to another reading in case you
don't find it."

No other reading was necessary. The next time Cicely visited
the Green she climbed the steps to her mother's house, making
her way over the tricycles, stuffed animals, bald-headed dolls
and collapsed balloons assembled by the children who have
kitchen and other privileges in that mansion. As she went up
two flights of stairs the banister rails were being polished by
descending small boys as she passed. She climbed the attic
stairs, but she was not yet as high as she could get. Luckily
there was a stepladder near the tall cabinet. On top of the
cabinet was a pillow covered in dark red satin, and beneath
it the silver in its maroon bags.

Berylla had, as usual, helped her neighbors.

Menu for a Clairvoyant Picnic

Casserole of Succotash *
Cinnamon Buns *
Labor Day Punch *
Brown Betty with Hard Sauce
Crowley Cheese

Succotash Casserole

In New England succotash means corn and shell beans, not limas. Corn and limas are good together when both are freshly picked, but the true succotash bean is the kind called Horticultural or Cranberry, with cranberry-sauce colored splashes on the pods. In 1954 both cranberry beans and golden bantam corn ripened before the frost and Mrs. Appleyard froze a good many packages. The beans were shelled and cooked until almost done and most of the water had cooked away. The corn was cut from the cob. Butter was melted in the frying pan and the corn was simmered in it with a finely scraped onion, a teaspoonful to a pint, for a few minutes. Very small beef cubes, tried out and crisply browned, were mixed with the beans, which were added, water and all, to the frying pan of corn.

Somehow there was more of this delicacy than Mrs. Appleyard remembered, and as spring made its grudging and gingerly advance she needed a little ingenuity to put it into circulation. Perhaps the best of these experiments was a large casserole that needed not only two packages of the succotash but two pints of tomato sauce to fill it; 1954 was a good tomato year too. The casserole was made by merely thawing out both the succotash and the tomato sauce in a large double boiler, transferring them to a casserole and topping the mixture with buttered Pepperidge Farm bread crumbs and thin slices of Cheddar cheese. By a tremendous effort Mrs. Appleyard here restrained herself from saying what she thinks about processed cheese. Instead she simply stated gently that she wants her cheese cut while she is looking at it from a large cheese she has tasted. She likes Crowley cheese, a zippy Vermont cheese, or mild Cheddar from Cabot in the same state, but she also has kind words to say about Cheddar from New York State and Wisconsin. No honest cheese need fear harsh words from this lady, but — well, perhaps we had better take up the tomato sauce.

Tomato Sauce

6 tablespoons olive oil
2 carrots, chopped
1 stalk of celery, chopped
2 tablespoons parsley, minced
cloves from one whole head of garlic, crushed
2 large onions, sliced thin
1 green pepper, chopped
2 quarts fine red tomatoes skinned and quartered

2 teaspoons light brown sugar
⅛ teaspoon cinnamon
½ teaspoon pepper from grinder
¼ teaspoon powdered thyme
½ teaspoon hot red pepper
2 cloves
salt to taste
1 quart chicken or beef stock
4 tablespoons butter

4 tablespoons flour

Put the olive oil into a large iron frying pan. Put everything into it except the tomatoes, flour and sugar. Stir over low heat till the onions are soft. Shove the vegetables aside, blend flour and fat. Add tomatoes, flour and sugar. Mix well, cover frying pan, set it into a slow oven, 300°, and let it simmer for an hour and a half. Stir it occasionally. Uncover it the last half hour. Strain it through a fine sieve, or use it as it comes. This will keep in the refrigerator, for years in the freezer. It is good with meat loaf, Hamburg Pie (p. 31) or Spaghetti Loaf (p. 115).

Cinnamon Buns (I.G.O.)

2 cups boiling water	8 cups sifted all-purpose flour
½ cup sugar	2 yeast cakes
1 teaspoon salt	¼ cup lukewarm water
¼ cup shortening	1 tablespoon sugar
2 eggs, well beaten	

Dissolve the sugar, salt and shortening in the boiling water. Cool to lukewarm. Dissolve the yeast cakes and 1 tablespoon sugar in the ¼ cup lukewarm water. Add to the first mixture. Add 4 cups of the flour. Add the eggs and the remainder of the flour. Stir thoroughly. Let rise in greased bowl in warm place till twice the bulk. Use at once or store for refrigerator rolls. For cinnamon buns roll out the dough, spread with brown sugar, cinnamon and butter, currants if desired. Roll up and cut in slices. Lay cut side down in greased pan. Let rise to double the bulk. Bake at 400° for 10–15 minutes depending on the size. Also good baked in individual cupcake pans.

Labor Day Punch

1 quart strong tea infusion made by boiling 2 tablespoons tea for 1 minute in 1 quart briskly boiling water and straining it.

6 lemons, thinly sliced, crushed with 2 cups sugar.
Add 1 quart cold water and let this stand in a cool place to mellow.
Use frozen fruit juice concentrates and make:

2 quarts orange juice   1 quart pineapple juice
2 quarts lemon juice   1 quart frozen strawberries
            ½ teaspoon mint extract

When you are ready to serve it put ice cubes in a large bowl, mix the tea and the fruit juices and pour them over the ice. Add the frozen strawberries and mint extract. Decorate the bowl with sprays of fresh mint.
This serves forty. It can be successfully refrozen for use another season.

Tea with the Fates

SUMMER could not really begin for Mrs. Appleyard without a visit to the Duncans. She has known them since they all had hair of reddish gold. It is white now, that shining white that has once been really golden. No one has yet invented a rinse that will produce this effect. Mrs. Appleyard once thought of making her fortune this way but has discarded the idea, along with woodcarving, plans for hunting for uranium and the imbedding of wildflowers in plastic.

There have to be a few things she doesn't do, she says reasonably. Using a Geiger counter among the Vermont hills would not be good for her blood pressure; the arrangement of violets and trilliums that she selected for her first experiment in plastic-as-an-art-form turned out so wry, withered and miserable that she threw it away at once. Twenty years ago she bought a set of woodcarving tools. This summer she tried them out and after half an hour put them back in the box, announcing that her instinct in never taking them out had been a sound one.

She has given up the project on which she meant to use them. It involved an old fanlight, a paneled door from Remember Appleyard's old house, discarded by Cicely in favor of three windows across the south front of this earliest house in Appleyard Center, and a good deal of co-operation from Roger Willard. As Roger is at present painting Mrs. Teasdale's addition, building a grape arbor for Geoffrey Toussaint and adjusting the plumbing here and there, this seemed like a pretty good time for Mrs. Appleyard not to be a woodcarver. Some mild surprise has been expressed by her friends at her having been defeated by anything. They wonder if she is feeling all right. Of course, an attack of common sense is likely to be painful, at whatever season it occurs. Otherwise she is in excellent health.

It was a fine cold bleak June day when she and Cicely started across country to see the Duncans. Wild apple trees were pink snowdrifts on pasture ledges. Pointed firs still cut black silhouettes against the thin new leaves on the hills. Brooks were full and foaming, ferns uncurling. Frost might still

scorch tomato vines, kill the bees before they fertilized the
apple blossoms, stunt the corn. Camilla rode with her mother
and grandmother as she had ridden each year since she was
a charcoal-eyed infant in the ancestral, pink-quilt-lined baby
basket in which all Cicely's babies had accompanied their
mother on social errands.

Frost or no frost, the Duncans had moved from their warm
apartment in Montpelier to the old yellow tavern in Spruce-
bury where Fiona has her antique shop in the high-ceilinged,
spring-floored dance hall in the ell. They had a good fire going
in the wood stove and they were making the biggest and handsomest braided rug Mrs. Appleyard had ever seen. They reminded her, she told them, a little of the Three Fates, a little
of an assembly line.

Fiona was choosing the materials from what she described
as "a lot of calamity" — a refined term for culch — and cutting them into narrow strips with her sharp, flashing shears.
Beatrice braided whatever was handed to her — maroon, green,
gray, black. Daisy sewed the braids, her needle moving with
butterfly swiftness. Unlike the Fates, who deal in prophecy,
they spoke of the past as they worked — of who wore the
gray striped trousers and tore them on a barbed-wire fence,
of how the maroon tablecloth was scorched by a flatiron left
too long in one spot, of a smudge of paint on Beatrice's green
dress.

"There wasn't a thing wrong with my navy suit, except the
girls said I should have a new one to go to legislature," said
Daisy, attaching a dark blue braid neatly to a gray one.

Daisy dresses in the utmost simplicity, yet suggests lavender
and old lace. She is small, daintily precise, brave and sensible
about the larger perils, terrified of mice, spiders and thunder-

storms. Unless you read about her in *Life* you would never guess that she is the oldest woman legislator in the country. If there were about a hundred more like her, equitably apportioned, the affairs of the nation, so Mrs. Appleyard thinks, would be carried on with far more efficiency and economy, although bounties on wildcats would jump several dollars, that being Daisy's special legislative interest.

The rug was getting so large that it was a long journey round it.

"Time to stop for the day, girls," Fiona said with a final click of her shears, and the assembly line went out of action as though a switch had been pulled.

Mrs. Appleyard went up with Fiona into the antique shop and inspected the newest treasures and some that she has been coveting for some time. Possibly her resistance was lowered by the winter cold that still seemed to linger in the old ballroom with its coved ceiling and its rows of small-paned windows. She resisted purple glass and pink luster teacups and ivory chessmen, but came downstairs looking guilty and clutching a large pastel of four warmly shawled and crinolined ladies said to be the Four Seasons. From the ten-cent table Camilla had chosen a walnut shell lined with thin blue silk and concealing a pair of china dolls half an inch long under a blanket of pinked flannel.

By the time they got downstairs again Daisy was setting the table with the thin silver teaspoons and the white gold-banded teacups. Beatrice had retired to her painting room and was at work on a ghostly white horse pulling an empty sleigh through whirling snow. Pictures finished and unfinished leaned against the walls. There is nothing of wild artistic disorder in Beatrice's studio. She paints as tidily in her hotel bedroom as in this big room with its sleigh bed and brightly papered walls.

Beatrice's pictures are full of lively figures. In the old dance hall, now the antique shop, girls in fluffy dresses kick up their heels while a tall fiddler saws on his violin and his dumpy wife thrums her harp. Outside the red schoolhouse you can almost hear the children squealing as sleds whizz down the hill and skaters trip each other up. Here is an eerie pond by moonlight. Branches of a great black tree writhe across the moon and a fire blazes on the ice. The figures round it have the air of being ghosts of skaters.

There is a blind man in many of the pictures. He stands still with his stick poised and listens to the laughter. Here he has left the skating party and moved to the tropics. There is a tree of life heavy with bright birds on the hill above him. Father Time is moving along briskly with his scythe like any last-century farmer behind in his haying. Has he just cut the ground from under the feet of the young lady in the brown and yellow redingote? She seems to be floating up toward the tree, but perhaps it is only that her parasol is acting like a parachute in reverse.

The blind man is outside the white church too, listening to the guests at the June wedding as the bridal party drive away in the fringed carryall drawn by the ghostly white horse, the ringing of the bell in the crooked steeple and the cows cropping the grass among the tombstones. He is at the barn-raising where he can hear the hammers and smell the boiled dinner.

Mrs. Appleyard smells something delicious too and she, Cicely and Camilla are asked to share it, although Daisy, who is folding over a perfect omelet, assures her that it isn't a meal at all, just a snack.

"I'm afraid to cook for you," she says, and looks so much

as if she meant it that Mrs. Appleyard hastens to tell her that all this talk about her being an epicure is a lot of nonsense.

"I'm just as likely as anyone else to have a cold lamb sandwich for lunch and eat it walking around the kitchen," she says. "I am merely the most appreciative eater that is likely to drop in. Do I really smell asparagus? And popovers? And don't tell me Fiona has whipped up a deep dish rhubarb pie! What is this — the Garden of Eden?"

After the snack they set to work at the rug again.

"Fiona planned it," said Daisy. "She's really a genius at planning."

"It's lucky I'm a genius at something." Fiona laughs good-naturedly. "It gets kind of monotonous hearing how remarkable Daisy and Beatrice are."

"We'd never get anywhere without you," Beatrice says.

They are in one of their mutual-admiration moods, Mrs. Appleyard notices, and waits for the tart comment that often varies it. It's a sound principle, she thinks, rather like serving pickles with maple sugar on snow.

"I'd have been up to see you," Beatrice says, "but the girls keep me right at my painting. They used to love to have me help in the kitchen. It would be 'Beatrice, you do make such lovely sponge cake,' or 'nobody can do bacon as well as you can.' Now it's 'don't think of washing a dish, Bee. Just go right in and paint. You know you have to get Geoffrey Toussaint's picture finished.' Sometimes I'm sorry I ever took to painting, they're such slavedrivers."

She braided deftly as she spoke.

"I wish you'd tell Bee to finish her pictures better," Fiona says. "You have a lot of influence with her."

"I'd as soon tell Picasso how to paint," said Mrs. Appleyard hastily.

"We'd have gone round by your place before," Fiona says, "but Daisy thinks the road is too rough."

"Too rough for the way Fiona drives at night," Daisy asserts.

"Daisy's afraid of every ditch between here and Montpelier," Fiona says, clicking her shears rapidly.

"I'd rather be a coward on the road than brave in a ditch." Daisy flashes a twinkle from behind her glasses at Mrs. Appleyard. Her diamond rings and her needle flash too.

"Mr. Toussaint admired our rug, too," said Beatrice. "He wants one just like it, only twice as big. When he was here to breakfast Tuesday afternoon he as good as ordered it along with four paintings, one for each season."

"Do you usually serve breakfast in the afternoon?" Mrs. Appleyard raised one eyebrow slightly.

"Well," said Daisy, her needle poised like a dragonfly over her work, "he wanted to come to breakfast with us, so we said, yes, any time, and it turned out to be about four o'clock, wasn't it, Fiona?"

"Four twenty-seven we sat down," said Fiona. "Of course, we knew he usually gets up around noon, so we began to expect him about two. I figure his hours are about three times as long as ordinary people's. Still, we had a good time when he came. We always do."

"So do we," said Mrs. Appleyard. "It must be nearly four twenty-seven now, Cicely. Your children will be wondering where you are. How pleasant to be a grandmother and escape so much domination by the young."

"I wouldn't mind so much," sighed Cicely, "if only they wouldn't go out the minute I get home. Still, I suppose it's better than not being noticed at all."

The Appleyard ladies had said their goodbyes and expressed

their thanks before they thought of inquiring what the menu had been at the belated breakfast.

"Never mind," said Cicely on the way home. "I shall make one up." So she did.

Menu for a High Tea

Omelet with Minced Chives and Parsley
Asparagus with Horse-radish and Sour Cream *
Popovers
Mousse au Chocolat *

Asparagus with Horse-radish and Sour Cream

Cook the asparagus either in full length stalks or broken into short pieces. Pour a little melted butter over it or pass with it the following sauce:

Mix a tablespoon of powdered horse-radish with a little sweet cream. Heat a cup of sour cream over hot, not boiling water. Add salt and freshly ground pepper to taste and stir in the horse-radish. Have ready some coarse bread crumbs browned in butter. Put the sauce in a bowl and sprinkle the crumbs over the top of the sauce.

Mousse au Chocolat

1 package semi-sweet chocolate bits	6 egg yolks
	¼ cup water
6 egg whites	

Melt the chocolate bits over hot water, with the water and egg yolks, stirring all the time. Don't let the water touch the top part of the double boiler. Remove as soon as the chocolate melts. Now fold in the stiffly beaten egg whites until the mixture is thoroughly blended. Pile in small glass serving dishes. This will resemble closely the French dessert of the same name. A variation is to add a heaping tablespoonful of powdered coffee to the mixture over the hot water. Whipped cream can be added but rather paints the lily.

High Breakfast with a Genius

Orange-Banana Whip *
Grilled Bones *
Guacamole *
Tutti-frutti in Cream *

Orange-Banana Whip

The menu that Cicely imagined for Geoffrey Toussaint's entertainment was probably not at all like the one that the Duncan sisters provided for him, but she felt that hers would have catered to some of his more Oriental tastes.

Orange-Banana Whip is made by combining one can of frozen concentrated orange juice, one can of water, ¼ cup dried non-fat milk and 1 ripe banana in the electric blender and running the blender for about 1 minute. Full of nourishment and vitamins.

Grilled Bones

"I always hoped I'd have a grilled bone some day," Geoffrey Toussaint had said wistfully.

Mrs. Appleyard was delighted to know of this yearning. She felt great happiness at the idea of being able to fulfill a wish for Geoffrey, that scatterer of gifts, who travels in a haze of electric frying pans, chiffon stoles, circus tickets for entire families, sets of china, books on psychic phenomena, albums of long-playing records — all wittily inscribed, all flying away from him by centrifugal force.

"I will use the short ribs from the roast of beef we had yesterday," she said, and fell to making the sauce, thus:

For four people:

8 short ribs of beef from a 14-pound roast
2 tablespoons flour
2 tablespoons butter
1 onion minced
1 tablespoon parsley, minced
¼ teaspoon fresh ground pepper
¼ teaspoon cayenne
¼ teaspoon nutmeg
2 cups hot beef or chicken stock
2 tablespoons beef fat and cracklings from it
2 tablespoons tomato ketchup
4 teaspoons Gulden's mustard
2 tablespoons Worcestershire sauce
1 teaspoon curry powder
½ teaspoon chili powder
4 tablespoons flour
salt to taste
1 cup beef jelly from the roast

Put the 4 tablespoons flour into a paper bag. Put in the bones and shake them until they are thoroughly coated. Lay them on a plate. You will need your largest frying pan for the bones and a smaller one for the sauce. Into the smaller pan melt the butter and cook the onion till it is soft. Lower the heat and rub the 2 tablespoons flour mixed with the dry seasonings with the butter. When it is well browned pour on the hot stock slowly and blend it in well. Add the ketchup, Worcestershire sauce and mustard and the beef jelly saved from the roast.

In the meantime, in the larger pan, cracklings cut from the roast have been trying out over a low flame. Put in the floured beef bones and brown them on all sides. This takes about 8 minutes. When you are ready to serve them, pour the sauce over them, adding a little more hot stock if the sauce seems too thick. Sprinkle the parsley over them.

There is very little meat on the bones but what there is of it is good with the sauce. Rice, mashed potato, or Yorkshire Pudding (p. 221) are all good to soak up the sauce.

Guacamole

This can also be made in the blender although it is not necessary to do so. Mash together 1 well-ripened avocado, 1 finely chopped green pepper, 1 finely chopped tomato, 1 small grated onion. Season with salt, pepper and cayenne. Stir in 1 tablespoon olive oil and ½ tablespoon lemon juice.

Tutti-Frutti

Cut in small pieces with scissors:

½ pound pitted dates   ½ pound figs
½ pound apricots   ¼ pound pitted prunes
¼ pound golden raisins
1 pint heavy cream

Soak for several hours in 1½ cups honey and ½ cup lemon juice. Just before serving, whip 1 pint heavy cream, flavor with ½ teaspoon almond extract and 3 tablespoons brandy; add to fruit mixture. Add 1 cup broken walnut meats or almonds. Chill and serve.

All these three dishes are *terribly healthy*. They also taste good.

July

Fan Mail

I N RESPONSE to those well-bred mystery stories she writes, Mrs. Appleyard has always received a certain amount of fan mail. She is not like Geoffrey Toussaint who has to employ a secretary to answer admiring letters about his books and to keep his accounts. Mrs. Appleyard never has any great difficulty in keeping her accounts except the usual ones about subtraction and a certain unjustified optimism about her finances when the Director of Internal Revenue forgets to cash her last check. She wonders if he is keeping her autograph on the June one for a souvenir.

Mrs. Appleyard takes this way of letting him know that she will be delighted to autograph anything she receives, that is, if the return postage is prepaid, by an early mail. She makes no charge for this service and wants him to understand that the item in her tax return — "Answering Fan Mail, $1.64" — is just for those replies where postage was not enclosed. As a matter of fact she had several other letters where it was.

It was one hot evening in July that she received her first letter from Horace. It was written in a most scholarly hand, postmarked Appleyard Center and dated Cranberry Hill. Now Cranberry Hill is where Geoffrey Toussaint lives. Cranberries are scarce there but poets, composers and painters are as thick as devil's paintbrush.

Which was Horace? Mrs. Appleyard wondered.

It was a somewhat petulant letter, differing from her on the proper method of cooking Hearts of Artichoke à la Princesse Lointaine. Now the truth of the matter is that when Mrs. Appleyard is writing a murder mystery she gives her imagination free rein about the food. If there ever were any artichokes cooked in the manner of a faraway princess with asparagus and pâté de Périgord and a sauce of sweetbreads and champagne it is one of the most purely coincidental coincidences that ever attended a murder in good society. Still, Horace, that was how he signed himself, seemed to have strong opinions on this dish. She had left out the cardamom seeds, he said. It was not thus, he added, that things were done in Provence.

He seemed to be taking a course in the works of Appleyard, because next day he spoke, more in sorrow than in anger, on the topic of Frangipani Cream. Why, he asked, inject New England rum into that delicate harmony of macaroons and orange flowers? Didn't she know that it originated in seventeenth century Italy? No wonder there was a murder. And he was sincerely hers, Horace.

That was Tuesday. On Wednesday he took up Bouillabaisse. If she had eaten it in Marseilles she would know that the saffron should be added only during the last five minutes, he wrote. Mrs. Appleyard, who by this time was wishing she had never given her characters anything more exotic than a peanut butter sandwich to eat, decided that steps must be taken to penetrate Horace's disguise.

"What," she asked Mary Angell, the postmistress, "are the names of the professors who are staying up on Cranberry Hill?"

She had hit the mark the first time. Their names were Douglas Wright and Horace Carter.

Mrs. Appleyard then produced a letter, directed with unusual legibility to "Horace, Appleyard Center, Vermont," and asked Mary to put it in the appropriate box. The letter was a challenge to Horace to settle his differences with her with, so to speak, egg beaters at twenty paces. The menus were to be constructed by each submitting dishes of certain categories. Slips bearing the names would be drawn by some neutral eater, if any such pusillanimous individual could be found in Appleyard Center. Each could enlist the services of not more than two assistants, and two or more guests could be invited. The different rounds in the tournament would be held at the houses of the contestants and would continue until one of them cried "Hold! Enough!"

Horace agreed to the terms, and succulent aromas of simmering and baking were soon blended with the scent of newmown hay. Mrs. Appleyard began hostilities one warm evening with salmon in tomato aspic with watercress and green mayonnaise. Brown bread sandwiches with cream cheese and garlic, new potatoes and peas in cream with beef cracklings were served with this. Patience Barlow, summoned to her neighbor's aid, constructed a Lady Baltimore cake as light as milkweed fluff. Venetia Hopkins contributed some of her own raspberries to go with it.

Horace, who turned out to be less severe in person than on paper, had no word of condemnation for this menu. He even admitted that it might be possible to cook sweetbreads without cardamom seeds. It was rather generally admitted that Mrs. Appleyard had won the first round. However, when the tournament was moved to Cranberry Hill, Horace Carter triumphed. He made Mrs. Appleyard eat tripe and like it!

The meal began with a French pâté de foie gras, generously truffled in a way Mrs. Appleyard has not seen since the first World War. When asked how such a treasure was acquired in the neighborhood of Cranberry Hill, Mr. Carter said that he had brought it with him from France on his last visit and had been carrying it around with him in case he met anyone who would appreciate it. Proud of having been found worthy of such a talisman, Mrs. Appleyard enthusiastically ate the main course: perfectly cooked polenta containing a number of delicious flavors and textures. She did not discover until she was eating Zuppa Inglese for dessert that one of the ingredients of the sauce for the polenta had been tripe. She hereby withdraws any earlier harsh remarks she has made about this substance, though she still thinks it should be cooked with discretion, preferably by Horace Carter.

Supper Menus for Hot Evenings on the Lawn

Iced Vichyssoise
Salmon in Tomato Aspic * with Watercress and Green
  Mayonnaise *
Brown Bread Sandwiches with Cream Cheese and Garlic
New Potatoes and Peas in Cream *
Lady Baltimore Cake *
Fruit Cup *

Pâté de Foie Gras with Truffles
Green Garden Soup
Polenta with Tripe in Tomato Sauce
Tossed Salad
Zuppa Inglese

Salmon in Tomato Aspic

The inspiration for this adventure with salmon in aspic was a copper mold in the shape of a fish. It was hanging on the wall in Venetia Hopkins' kitchen where it presented a handsome appearance. Mrs. Appleyard was in one of her "let's make something we never made before" moods when her eye encountered the fish. Up to that time its owner had probably thought of it as a decorative piece of still life. Soon everything was in motion and Mrs. Appleyard was murmuring incantations over a kettle of court bouillon. If you are going to make this dish, she suggests that you start the day before if you are going to serve it for lunch, or early in the morning if supper is your goal. You will need for a large mold:

3 pounds of Penobscot or Gaspé
   salmon
salmon bones
1 carrot
1 onion
a small piece of bay leaf, a sprig
   of thyme, parsley, pepper, salt
   to taste
fresh tarragon leaves, peppercorns

1 lemon
1 quart tomato juice
2 envelopes plain gelatin
2 eggs, hard-boiled
oak leaf lettuce
egg shells for clearing soup. (If
   you didn't make sponge cake
   or soufflé that day, use two
   egg whites.)

Make the court bouillon, using the carrot, onion, thyme, bay leaf and parsley, salmon bones and two quarts of water. Cook them all together for half an hour. Strain through cheesecloth over the fish. A Dutch oven of heavy aluminum or iron or an electric frying pan is a good container; something in which the fish can be simmered gently for about 40 minutes. Now remove the fish and put it aside to cool. Add the tomato juice to the bouillon and cook it down until there is about a quart. Add the peppercorns the last few minutes of cooking: they turn bitter if cooked too long. Add the egg shells. If you do not have plenty with some white clinging to them, add one or two extra whites. When the whites are cooked hard, strain the bouillon again through cheesecloth.

Soak the gelatin in the juice of the lemon and a little cold water for a few minutes. Pour the hot bouillon over the mixture and stir until the gelatin is dissolved. Wet the fish mold with cold water. Pour in a little of the jellied bouillon, lay six tarragon leaves crossed on top of it and set the mold into the refrigerator. While it is getting stiff, remove the skin and bones from the fish and peel and slice the hard-boiled eggs.

When the jelly has stiffened, lay the egg slices around the

sides of the mold and put in the fish. Mrs. Appleyard tries to have the fish look as if it came in one piece and was really curved in the sportive fashion indicated by the outlines of the mold. Now pour in the rest of the jellied bouillon and set the mold in the refrigerator. Your only problem now is to get it out of the mold intact the next day.

Have your best silver platter ready and plenty of fresh parsley and sliced lemon at hand. Set the fish mold in a pan of warm, *not hot* water. Watch it. In a minute you will see the first softening of the jelly around the edge. Remove the mold immediately from the water. Wipe it dry. Put the platter over it and turn the whole thing upside down. (This is the only kind of exercise Mrs. Appleyard really enjoys.) If the jellied fish does not leave the mold immediately, wring a cloth dry out of hot water and apply it to the top of the mold. Just when you think it is never coming out, it will. Lift off the mold. Surround the fish with the oak leaf lettuce, parsley and sliced lemon, and the green mayonnaise. Put it where it will keep cold and take a deep breath.

Green Mayonnaise

The easy way to make this is in the electric blender. However, you have Mrs. Appleyard's permission to chop and purée the greens in the way you find most convenient. You need only a fourth of a cupful, so it is not a very exhausting task. She puts into the blender:

2 tablespoons of lemon juice
¼ cup chopped greens — a little watercress, parsley, a leaf or two of spinach, a slice or two of a scallion or a slice of onion

Run the blender until you have some bright green pulp. Add:

1 whole egg
¼ cup oil (olive oil or part olive, part salad oil)
dry seasonings: mustard, pep-per, salt to your taste, which she is willing to bet is not hers, sugar

Run the blender about five seconds or until everything is well blended.

Now add, a small amount at a time, ¾ cup oil.

Run five seconds after each addition. Run a few seconds after the last oil is added.

Use the same method, only with longer beating, with the electric mixer. If you do it by hand, it is very convenient if someone will beat while you pour the oil. This is called executive ability. Non-executives get someone else to pour the oil while they beat. It took Mrs. Appleyard about forty years to find this out. Sometimes it seems as if she were not awfully bright.

New Potatoes and Peas in Cream

This dish is something like a transit of the sun and Jupiter. The ingredients for it — if it is to be perfect — do not come together every fine summer day by any means. The potatoes should be so young and innocent that they are not much bigger than golf balls. The peas should be no larger than good-sized pearls and they should be picked no longer than twenty minutes before they are cooked. The cream — but perhaps we had better not listen to Mrs. Appleyard on the subject of cream. Incidentally, we have known that lady to construct a fair approximation of this delicacy out of some potatoes from a neighboring state, peas she found in her freezer with a date in her own handwriting two years earlier and cream from a cow born and raised outside Vermont. She used to make it with salt pork but has now changed to beef cracklings and thinks the flavor is more subtle.

For six people you will need:

18 potatoes the size of golf balls (about 2 quarts)	1 onion finely minced
1 quart of shelled peas	¼ pound beef cracklings made from the fat of roast beef or
1 cup thick cream	steak

Begin by cutting the beef fat into half-inch cubes and set them over a very low flame to try out. Stir them occasionally and pour off some of the fat. Save this in a marked jar. Nothing is so good for browning hashed brown potatoes. The cubes should shrink to half their size and be a delicate tan in color. Mrs. Appleyard, who used to cook new potatoes and peas in cream in several separate pans and serve them in a Bennington bowl, has now become so dashingly modern that she recommends doing the whole thing in a frying pan or a Dutch enamel dish that comes right to the table. She likes the dish — a pale green one — best but says they taste all right out of a scarlet and ivory frying pan too.

When the cracklings are almost ready, put in the onion and cook till it is pale yellow. Don't let it brown. Turn off the heat while you are scrubbing the potatoes. You don't peel them. Add them to the contents of the dish, pour in some boiling water, not too much: you want most of it to cook away. Let them cook partly covered so that the steam will escape while you are shelling the peas — about 20 minutes.

When they are almost done and the water has mostly disappeared, add the peas. They should cook in 5 minutes. Stir them well into the potatoes. When they are tender but not mushy, add the cream. Let it just come to the boil. Turn off the heat, cover the dish and leave it to mellow a few minutes.

This is a good thing to serve when you are wondering if there is enough cold beef to go around, or even if you are not considering anything of the sort.

Lady Baltimore Cake

Mrs. Appleyard, not being strong on arithmetic, hesitates to say just how long ago it was that she ate her first piece of Lady Baltimore cake. Even though her culinary triumphs up to that time had consisted entirely of one rather scorched pan of fudge, she sat down immediately with her hostess's manuscript cookbook and copied down the receipt in an innocent and strangely legible hand. Something must have warned her that half a century or so later Horace Carter would be coming to supper.

Naturally such an emergency led to a good deal of discussion between Mrs. Appleyard and Patience Barlow. It was felt by both ladies that the occasion demanded something really stupendous, historic, monumental — served, of course, as nonchalantly as if they launched such delicacies upon the world every day. They turned over instructions for various types of guided missiles until at last Mrs. Appleyard announced, in a tone familiar to her family, a tone prophetic yet wistful, rather like that of a tiger about to spring upon a water buffalo: "I have never made this before."

Patience, recognizing that destiny had spoken, promptly got out three 10-inch layer cake tins and the fun began.

There are three stages involved in making a Lady Baltimore and unless you feel like devoting most of a day to it, Mrs. Appleyard advises you to get a package of somebody's cake mix and relax.

First you make the cake batter, then you make a syrup, last you make the frosting and filling.

Batter

1¼ cups butter	2½ cups sugar
5 large eggs	1¼ cups milk
4⅓ cups sifted flour	5 teaspoons baking powder
2¼ teaspoons almond extract	2½ teaspoons vanilla

Grease 3 large layer cake pans with Spry. Sift the flour four times with the baking powder. Light the oven at 350°. Even if the electric mixer was invented long after Lady Baltimore it is all right to use it, Mrs. Appleyard says. Cream butter and sugar. Break in the eggs one at a time and beat well. Beat in the flour alternately with the milk, using the rubber scraper to keep the batter away from the sides. Add the flavoring. Put the batter in the greased pans. Bake 30 minutes, reducing the heat to 325° after the first ten minutes if the layers are browning too quickly.

Now make the syrup.

1¼ cups sugar	¾ cup water
½ teaspoon almond extract	½ teaspoon vanilla

This should cook until it is rather thick. Don't let it discolor. Take your layers out of the pans and spread them with the warm syrup while they are still warm. This keeps the frosting, which you will now make, from making the layers soggy.

Lady Baltimore Frosting

The night before you are going to make the cake, mix:

3 cups seeded raisins, cut fine	1 cup sliced blanched almonds
2 cups chopped pecans	15 figs cut in small pieces
½ cup candied cherries	

and cover with ½ cup brandy, 1 teaspoon vanilla, 1 teaspoon almond, 1 tablespoon lemon juice. Stir occasionally so that all the fruit will absorb a little liquid.

Beat three egg whites until they make firm peaks.

Mix 1 cup water, 3 teaspoons corn syrup and 3 cups sugar. Boil together until it makes a firm soft ball — 234°.

Pour the syrup slowly on the beaten egg whites and get someone else to keep beating them all the time. Add the fruit and nuts. Spread between the layers, on top of the cake and around the sides. Do this on the cake plate on which you serve it, covering the plate first with four triangles of wax paper, points toward the center, which you will pull out when the frosting has had time to set.

Fruit Cup
DESSERT FOR A HOT EVENING

Mrs. Appleyard thinks that the fresh fruit that comes all cut up in glass jars is a great alleviation to anyone who has bursitis or is even, like herself, just plain lazy.

(One of her relatives who was looking over her shoulder as she was writing these remarks murmured: "And so I suppose was Napoleon. Also Susan B. Anthony, Thomas Alva Edison and Theodore Roosevelt!")

Take a quart jar of fruit, Mrs. Appleyard continued imperturbably, and a package of frozen melon balls. Anyone who is energetic enough to cut melon balls is welcome to do so, she added. Now mix

½ cup white wine
2 tablespoons lemon juice
strained juice from 1 cup fresh
   raspberries crushed with 2
   tablespoons sugar

3 drops peppermint extract
sprigs of fresh mint

Combine the fruit and melon balls. Mix the other ingredients except the sprigs of mint, pour over the fruit and set the bowl into the refrigerator for the flavors to blend. When you serve it, put a sprig of mint into each cup.

Mallets and Balls

It was in July that the croquet tournament broke out. Every summer since the lawn was leveled and graded in 1925 the croquet set has been put out on the side porch. Every autumn what is left of it has been carried back into the woodshed. At present it consists of portions of two sets, one perhaps five years younger than the other, but both so weathered by rain and sun that it is hard to tell the green ball from the brown one.

Some colors are missing entirely, the balls having been cloven in twain, the shafts of the mallets split, by players who confused croquet and golf. However, there is enough equipment left so that Mrs. Appleyard's grandchildren can still, in moments of irritation, threaten each other with the same mallets used for that purpose by their parents. Balls can still bounce off the well-rusted wickets or miss by a hair's breadth the broken-topped stakes. They can still disappear into the raspberry bushes and turn up next spring, their stripes fainter than ever. The old arguments can still arise.

It is a long time since Mrs. Appleyard has had a mallet in her hand, and it was a happy surprise to her to find, one hot evening while she was serving supper on the lawn, that she could still occasionally send a ball through a wicket. She also made several brilliant hits, as unexpected to her opponents as to herself, and missed the easiest shots by wide margins. She was, in short, in her usual form.

Oddly enough, she and her partner, Colin Dalzell, the composer, did not win. They did, however, give the champions, Venetia Hopkins and Kendall Royce, a battle of a spirited sort. This began soon after the hummingbirds had left the larkspur, continued while the hermit thrushes were singing in the woods across the pond and lasted until the fireflies were doing their best to illuminate the croquet ground. Unfortunately there were not enough of them on duty, and before the match was over the players were using cigarette lighters to find their balls. Mrs. Appleyard had the interesting idea of marking the wickets with luminous tape, the kind used on the rear bumper of her car. She thought it would shine in reflected firefly and starlight. She was mistaken.

A better illuminated match was held at Kendall Royce's the next week. When the guests arrived they drove under an arch made by a yellow banner stretched between two pine trees. There were bright blue letters on the banner, saying "Welcome, Cranberry Hill Croquet Meet, 1955."

The Royce croquet set was new and shining. Balls, mallets and stakes displayed the proper colors. The course, however, had some unusual features. One was a small hill near the second stake. The player who hit his ball too gently saw it reach the top and roll back to his feet. Hit too hard, the ball traveled along the ridge and downhill into the goldenrod. Even Cicely had trouble with a hollow near the center wicket, and her partner, who was trying in vain to hit a ball that was resting in the hollow, could be heard chanting in a tone of resentful disgust: "It hopped right over it! It hopped right over it!"

Naturally, with the emotional and physical strains produced by croquet under these conditions, sustaining food is needed. Kendall Royce had filled a big ironstone tureen with a seafood bisque, rich with cream, chopped clams, shrimp and lobster, garnished with parsley, chives and slivered almonds. With it he served French bread spread with garlic butter, dusted with sharp cheese and paprika. The salad in its huge wooden chopping tray held all the young vegetables and lettuces that his garden could provide — radish roses, tiny raw peas, carrots and green beans, loose-leaf lettuces soft as butter, head lettuce dark and crisp, bitter chicory, bland watercress from his brook.

By dessert time the players were back at the course, bite-size mince and apple turnovers in their hands and the red wine punch floating its cucumber circles in the big brown mixing bowl within easy reach. Cicely and Carleton Welch were playing a final challenge round with Venetia Hopkins and Kendall Royce. Cicely had, by bitter experiment, learned the nasty intricacies of Kendall's course and was displaying the same sort of terrifying virtuosity which had made her undisputed champion of Appleyard Center at fifteen.

"You are too nice," she said to Kendall as she drove his ball into the dusk of the pine grove. "In this game it is the least pleasant person who wins." She took her ball and Carleton's the length of the course in a single turn and banged them both against the stake as the first stars pricked through deepening sky.

It was thought later that it was this display by Cicely of ruthless skill that caused her paying guest, a pink-cheeked, stiff-gestured young Englishman, much taken, by his own account, with the vitality of American civilization, to pack his bags and leave suddenly by the noon train the following day. The note he left on the bureau said that, frankly, he was bored. The other croquet players, however, subscribe to the theory that he was shocked by an excess of American vitality.

MORE MENUS FOR SUPPER ON THE LAWN

Seafood Bisque *
Garlic Bread
Tossed Salad, French Dressing *   Cheese Cubes *
Red Wine Punch
Mince or Apple Turnovers
Coffee

Cold Borschtch
Caged Lobster *
Green Garden Salad *
Corn Dodgers *
Fresh Peaches in Brandy *
Coffee

Tomachicko *
Veal and Ham Pie *
   with Two-Thousand-Layer Pastry *
Lettuce Salad * (Five Kinds), French Dressing
Scalded Johnnycake
Coffee Angel Cake *
Lemon and White Wine Punch (Croquet Cooler)*

Seafood Bisque

For six servings take:

1 can minced clams	1 diced onion
1 pound lobster meat	1 stalk of celery, cut up
1 pound shrimp	½ cup blanched almonds
	parsley, chives

Cook them slowly and lightly in butter for about 5 minutes. Make a white sauce with 3 tablespoons butter, 2 tablespoons flour, 2 cups milk, 1 cup cream. Season with a little cayenne pepper, add a little diced pimento, salt to taste. Reheat the shellfish in the bisque — do not boil. Just before serving add ½ cup blanched almonds cut in slivers. Sprinkle with chopped chives and parsley. Serve in a big tureen.

French Dressing for Tossed Salad

¾ cup olive oil	salt to taste
¼ cup red vinegar in which you have soaked a clove of garlic	½ teaspoon dry mustard
	¼ teaspoon curry powder
	ground pepper
1 teaspoon paprika	1 teaspoon Worcestershire sauce
1 teaspoon sugar	1 medium onion, diced

Put everything in a screw-top jar and shake well. Chill. Just before you serve it, strain it and add 1 teaspoon each of parsley, tarragon and chives, finely chopped.

Cheese Cubes to go with Tossed Salads

You will need unsliced bread, homemade or Pepperidge Farm, for these.

3 slices of bread ¾ inch thick	4 teaspoons melted butter
1 egg, beaten	1 cup dry dairy cheese, grated

Cut the crust off the bread and cut it into ¾-inch cubes. Mix the egg and melted butter. Dip the cubes into the mixture and then roll them in grated cheese. Put them on a buttered baking sheet and bake them at 375° until they start to brown — 6 or 7 minutes.

It will be better for all concerned if you double the rule.

Caged Lobster — Vermont

To get to Vermont, lobsters need wings. Luckily this is no trick at all to the hardy Green Mountain airmen. They always seem ready to dash over to the Maine coast, snatch a load of lobsters and zoom back while their freight is still aggressive enough to snap each other's claws off. An episode over which Vermonters have done a little boasting, in a quiet refined way, of course, occurred when chefs from all over New England got together and cooked lobster for a jury of old experienced lobster eaters. The Vermont version was pronounced the best. Encouraged by this victory, Mrs. Appleyard tells how she fixes lobster in the only New England state without a sea coast.

Winged lobsters, she says, naturally need cages. You begin

by making them out of homemade unsliced bread. They should be four inches long, three inches wide and two inches high. You will have a by-product of a good many bread crumbs. Mrs. Appleyard at such times is not in a mood to care what you do with them.

Hollow out the bread, leaving a thickness of half an inch at sides and bottom. Butter the cages thinly all over, inside and out, with softened butter. Set them in the oven for a few minutes until they are slightly brown. Don't brown them too much — they are going back later.

Now make whichever you prefer: lobster Newburg, creamed lobster, lobster salad by your favorite rule. The sauce should not be too thin. In any event, fill the cases with the mixture, put mayonnaise on top of the lobster, set them on a baking sheet until the mayonnaise browns and puffs. You will not need anything else to eat for quite a while.

Variations: The boxes may be filled with creamed crabmeat and mushrooms, with chicken salad, or creamed chicken and mushrooms — in fact whatever you like. An easier method is to use hard dinner rolls, hollowed out, brushed with butter, filled and heated through.

Green Garden Salad

This is a local version of Caesar Salad and it occurs as soon as there are several kinds of lettuce ready in the garden. Mrs. Appleyard always plants several varieties because the descriptions in the catalogue are so ingeniously tempting. It is a literary feat she greatly admires, she says, to make you think one kind of lettuce is really going to taste different from another.

Fortunately they do actually look different, and an enormous old wooden bowl, one of the oblong kind once used for working butter, is a handsome sight when it is filled with a variety of shapes and colors.

Mrs. Appleyard likes to combine the long greenish-white leaves of romaine, the soft clusters of oak leaf with their deeply indented edges, crip bunches of iceberg that bear little resemblance to the tasteless tennis balls wrapped in cellophane of the winter season. There are darker greens too — Big Boston, Black-seeded Simpson, rosettes of bronze-tinged Mignonette, Matchless with leaves like a deer's tongue. At least the catalogue says so. Mrs. Appleyard has never seen a deer's tongue and bases her impressions solely on the slender pointed leaves of Matchless.

Another kind of lettuce said to be especially sweet and succulent is Bibb, which is also said to be a gourmet's favorite. The inner leaves are creamy yellow. Gourmet Appleyard cannot really detect anything very subtle about its flavor but admits that it is decorative in the salad bowl. She does not wish to enforce any of these varieties on those who have their own favorites but simply says mildly that one charm of this salad lies in its being made of several kinds of lettuce, well washed, well dried, and that one of them should be romaine. Also she states that she knows that it is the custom to tear the leaves for this salad into convenient pieces. However, with lettuce picked early in your own garden, leaf by leaf, this is not necessary. She chooses small leaves, cutting them off with scissors. This method leaves roots and dirt in the garden and brings only the lettuce into the kitchen. So, for six people:

1 large bowl of various kinds of lettuce including romaine
1 cup olive oil (part salad oil if you prefer)
1 whole raw egg
juice of 1 lemon (2 tablespoons)
peppercorns in a grinder
salt to taste
1 teaspoon dry mustard, ¼ teaspoon cayenne, ¼ teaspoon sugar
1 teaspoon paprika
½ cup dry cheese grated
4 slices Pepperidge Farm bread ¾ inch thick, crusts cut off
chopped chives and minced parsley if you have them growing
garlic — at least 4 good "ears," "cloves," "beans" or whatever you call them. More if you like

Begin several hours before you are going to mix the salad by making some garlic oil. This is simply pouring a cup of oil over the peeled and sliced cloves of garlic and leaving it in a cool place. Now pick the lettuce, wash it, drain and dry it well, and put it into the lowest part of the refrigerator to chill and crisp. Slice the bread into ¾-inch cubes, chop the chives, mince the parsley. Now take the cheese, and mix it with the mustard and other dry seasonings except the pepper. If you have real Parmesan, use it. Mrs. Appleyard says any honest dry chunk of dairy cheese is better than imitation Parmesan flavored with monosodium glutamate. Better not uphold the virtues of this substance in that lady's hearing. Those are fighting words. She could say more but will get on with the salad.

Anyway it is now time to relax, smell the newly cut grass, clover, syringas, spice pinks. After all, this is summer. The salad is to be mixed when the guests are sitting down and ready for it. Just before they come, you gently fry the croutons in the garlic oil, using about a half of it, and then put them in a slow oven for a little while to dry out and crisp up.

First you begin by giving a slight nervous shock to those who have not been exposed to this salad before by breaking the raw egg over the greens. The purpose of this is to help the dressing to coat every leaf. Toss the leaves carefully, gently, till the egg disappears. Sprinkle in the chives and parsley. Keep tossing. Grind in plenty of pepper. Toss some more. Now add the oil and lemon juice, mixed together. If there are not 6 tablespoons of oil to 2 of lemon juice add some more oil. Keep lettuce moving. Every leaf should be coated and there should be no excess dressing in the bottom of the bowl. Mix in the cheese and other seasonings, still tossing. Last of all add the garlic croutons. By this time the guests are so hungry that they could eat two-weeks-old iceberg lettuce flavored with m-n-s-d-m gl-t-m-t-, but never mind. The hostess is happy anyway.

Corn Dodgers (F.G.B.)

3 cups boiling water	1 tablespoon butter
1 scant teaspoon salt	1 cup Indian meal

Add meal slowly to the boiling water, stirring carefully so it doesn't lump. Add butter and beat well. Drop by spoonfuls on buttered baking sheets. Bake 25 minutes or until puffed and lightly browned in a hot oven, 450°–475°.

They should be crisp outside and hot enough so that the soft part inside burns your tongue and melts butter. Incidentally, Mrs. Appleyard uses an extra tablespoonful of butter and dots some more on the top but — as a co-worker of hers was once heard to remark — "It's just as well to look the other way when she gets out the butter." She says honey is good on these johnnycakes — that's what they are; also maple syrup.

Fresh Peaches in Brandy

Peel the peaches, dipping them briefly in boiling water and, as soon as you have removed the skins, halve them and put them into a bowl containing a can of frozen lemonade concentrate diluted with one can of water. (This supplies both sugar and lemon juice to keep them from turning brown.) For six people allow nine large peaches. Add to the bowl ½ cup of brandy and 1 teaspoon of almond extract. Chill until you are ready to serve them.

Tomachicko
FOR A HOT EVENING

The last time you cooked a fowl you saved some of the stock, Mrs. Appleyard hopes. And cooked it down until it jellied when you chilled it? And you carefully skimmed off the fat? Good, you will be glad you did.

Slice up an onion. Pour 3 cups of tomato juice over it. Juice from your own tomatoes is best but canned will do. If you like other seasonings, add them, but don't overdo it: this is delicately flavored. Mrs. Appleyard thinks that one leaf of fresh basil, one of rosemary, one of tarragon are enough. Let it stand a couple of hours in the refrigerator. Then combine it with three cups of chicken stock, straining out the herbs and onions. This is good hot too.

Veal and Ham Pie

Mrs. Appleyard has recently worked out an improved technique for making this delicacy and hereby tells all. She began by putting into a large kettle the veal, chicken feet, bones and seasoning, carefully manicuring the chicken feet first, of course. They were a present from her butcher and no doubt yours would be equally generous. They add flavor to the broth and make it jelly easily. As the great feature of the pie is that the meat is surrounded by a sort of savory aspic, this is important. Perhaps some laggards in cookery might use gelatin. Mrs. Appleyard shuts her eyes to this suggestion and does not even attempt to estimate how much would be needed. Colburn's ham, a Montpelier product, is her favorite kind but your own favorite will do.

Take:

2 pounds veal cut from the leg	4 eggs, hard-boiled
1½-pound slice of Colburn's Vermont ham	½ teaspoon nutmeg
	½ teaspoon cinnamon
6 chicken feet	6 whole cloves
veal bones	½ teaspoon pepper
celery tops	3 onions, sliced
3 sprays of parsley	1 carrot, sliced

pastry (p. 93)

Put the ham on to simmer, removing all the fat you can, in a frying pan with plenty of water, which should be changed occasionally. The water is a good basis for split-pea soup and may be saved for those in a mood for such a dish. At the same time put on the veal, bones, chicken feet, seasonings, onion and carrot to simmer. While they are cooking she has plenty of time to make some Two-Thousand-Layer pastry (p. 93) and to be beaten at a couple of games of chess. At one time she used to bake the pastry on top of the pie. She now advocates baking a lid, neatly tailored to fit the top of the dish, and putting it on when the pie is served. This was a suggestion of Venetia's over the chess board — she said it was a pity to let the pastry lose any of its lightness and fragility by being baked with liquid under it and served cold. Mrs. Appleyard was so struck with this idea that she was checkmated soon afterwards and was able to give her complete attention to cooking.

After both veal and ham are tender, strain off the veal broth. Set it to cool, then put it into the freezer. Cut veal and ham into neat cubes. In a Pyrex dish, loaf size, arrange a layer of meat, hard-boiled egg slices against the side of the dish so they can be seen through the glass, then more meat and more eggs. Fill the dish with the rest of the meat. Now the broth should be cold enough so the fat can be easily removed. There should be about 4 cups. Pour it over the meat until the dish is well filled. Save out a cup of it and reduce it to half a cup. In the meantime set the dish, covered but not too tightly, into a 350° oven and cook until the meat and broth are well amalgamated — about forty minutes. Add the broth you have cooked down, set the dish in a cold place. When it is well chilled the spaces between the meat should be filled with sparkling savory aspic. Put the pastry lid on and serve it with a tossed salad.

Two-Thousand-Layer Pastry

4 cups flour (measured after sifting. Save what is left over to flour
  the board)
extra flour for rolling out, as little as possible
1 cup butter, very cold
1 cup lard, very cold
1 cup ice water

Put flour, butter and lard into a large wooden chopping
bowl. Have the chopping knife cold. Chop until butter and
lard are in cubes the size of your little finger tip. Add the
water half a cup at a time, blending it in with your chopper.
Now flour your pastry board and rolling pin. Get the paste
out of the bowl with the chopper and a spatula. Never touch
it with your hands.

Roll it out about ¾ inch thick. Cut it in thirds, using the
spatula and a chilled pancake turner. Pile the outside pieces
over the ones in the middle. Be gentle. Pastry hates rough
handling. Repeat the process seven times, turning the board
90 degrees each time. Your pastry will now have 2187 layers.
If you do not believe Mrs. Appleyard's arithmetic, you may
do the calculation yourself, but really you had better not take
your mind off the pastry. Have a chilled plate ready with
wax paper on it. Wrap the pastry up and chill it several hours
before using it. When you roll it out, add a few little dots of
butter to it to enrich the extra flour you used on your board
and rolling pin.

Bake it in a hot oven — 450°. This is so the air spaces between your layers will expand suddenly. When it begins to
brown, reduce the heat slightly. It takes about 45 minutes to

cook a pie with two crusts thoroughly, less for single crust pies or tarts. Good luck to you!

Coffee Angel Cake

Here is a good way, Mrs. Appleyard says, to disguise the fact that you did not make your angel cake yourself, some hot July morning, but sensibly bought it.

1 tablespoon plain gelatin, soaked in ¼ cup cold water
1 cup powdered sugar
8 egg yolks
1 teaspoon vanilla

1 teaspoon almond extract
2 tablespoons hot strong coffee
2 cups heavy cream
½ cup blanched and toasted almonds

Put the soaked gelatin in the top of a double boiler, add the coffee and when the gelatin is dissolved, the sugar. Cool. Beat the egg yolks until light and lemon colored. Add flavorings. Fold in gelatin mixture. Whip the cream and add it. Chill. Cut the angel cake in halves horizontally. Spread the coffee mixture between the layers and on the top and sides. Sprinkle the toasted almonds on top.

Croquet Cooler
(LEMON AND WHITE WINE PUNCH)

6 lemons, thinly sliced
2 cups sugar
1 tablespoon tea
1 quart boiling water

1 quart cold water
1 quart white wine
1 quart ginger ale
¼ cup mint leaves

sprigs of mint

Cover the sliced lemons with the sugar and crush them with a potato masher till the sugar dissolves. Add the mint leaves and crush gently. When the water boils, throw in the tea and boil exactly one minute. Strain over the lemon and sugar. Stir. Add the cold water. Set aside to cool and blend. An hour before serving time add the white wine, chilled. At serving time add the ginger ale and the sprigs of mint. No harm is done to anyone by floating a few strawberries in it.

The Hotter the Better

IT WAS during the visit of the Princess to Cranberry Hill that everyone started to serve curry so feverishly.

"Is there any other way to serve it?" inquired Geoffrey Toussaint, who happened to walk into the summer kitchen one afternoon, finding Mrs. Appleyard mixing cayenne pepper and curry powder with a lavish hand.

"I could easily make you some Cream of Wheat," Mrs. Appleyard replied hospitably. "I think you will find," she added, "that this tastes like curry."

"Now why don't you be more like your mother?" Geoffrey asked Cicely, who was valiantly chopping onions. "When I make a statement to you or ask you a question, you always come up with a contradiction or a brash answer that cuts the ground from under me. But your mother — I remember the first time I met her I said: 'The Albigensians were named after a bishop called Albi.' She went right on beating eggs for a Crème Brûlée and said, oh so gently: *'I think you will find* that they were named for a *place* called Albi.' And of course the Encyclopedia agreed with her."

"Most people ask me — 'and are you as clever as your mother?' " Cicely replied, wiping away her onion-inspired tears. "It's refreshing to meet someone who recognizes at once that I am not. The other question is so extremely difficult to answer without insulting somebody. How are you making curry this time, Mother?"

"The way the Princess taught me," Mrs. Appleyard said. "You'd have learned too if you hadn't gone to Cape Cod."

"Is the Princess the lady with the raven tresses I met sunning herself on your terrace, Geoffrey?" asked Cicely.

"She washed her hair every morning and then oiled it thoroughly after lunch. She's a better than average blues singer, but she's sadly deficient in yoga and Hindu philosophy," replied Geoffrey.

"Deficiencies which you could no doubt correct handily between lunch and dinner," Mrs. Appleyard said. "Are you finished with the onions, Cicely?"

"Did the Princess cook right here in this very kitchen?" asked Joan Bradshaw, Cicely's third child. "When I went to New York with her on the plane she wore a kind of brown sheet with pink showing through and gold all round the edge."

"That was her traveling costume," said her grandmother. "The evening she came here to make curry her sari — what you called a sheet — was white and gold. I thought of having the kitchen done over with mother-of-pearl tiles studded with an occasional ruby. Perhaps a few gold frying pans with turquoise handles. Too late now, though. Still, it was a pretty sight, just as it was. As though a Bird of Paradise had lighted on my white phlox.

"The curry was excellent," she added. "We didn't have anything with it except some of my 1954 chutney and some brown rice. She said I cooked the rice very nicely. That was my proudest moment."

"I went to a curry party where there were fresh frozen mangoes," Cicely said, "and fresh coconut. I believe some was combined with cucumbers and sour cream."

"That's fresh coconut in that bowl," her mother said.

"Where did you get it?" asked Cicely.

"I bought a coconut for fifteen cents and spent five dollars worth of time getting it open and grating it," Mrs. Appleyard replied. "Not to mention those gouges I made on the table while I was pounding it with a croquet mallet. It will take three hours to get them out with oil and pumice. I'm glad now," she added, stirring sour cream and coconut milk into the curry sauce, "that I never took my five favorite books and went to live on a desert island. I would have starved rather than deal with coconuts."

She tasted the sauce, added a trifle more curry powder and said, "There, I think that is almost good enough for the Princess."

It is generally agreed that if Mrs. Appleyard only had a suitable sari — something matronly in purple and gold — she would be able to turn out a highly acceptable curry. She has given up buying any gold frying pans but has brightened the summer kitchen with a set enameled with scarlet outside and ivory within. These are so handsome that she serves food right in them, placing them on wrought iron trivets on her well-polished table. By arranging these judiciously and setting out twelve dishes of condiments she is able to cover up most of the scars of the Battle of the Coconut.

"Your table," said Geoffrey Toussaint, who had moved a trivet, "has certainly received cruel and abrasive treatment."

Mrs. Appleyard mentioned her plan for eradicating the scars with linseed oil.

"Better add some of the curry sauce," suggested Mr. Toussaint, gasping for air. "That'll burn them off."

Weak spirits, Mrs. Appleyard says, may use half as much curry and cayenne as the Princess suggests.

No one died of internal combustion after Mrs. Appleyard's curry dinner, but those who vied with her in Oriental cookery did indeed modify the amount of spice in the sauce. Cicely produced a creditable minced beef and green pea curry which she claimed resembled one called "kofta" that she had eaten in an East Indian restaurant in England. (It was here that she encountered the menu which had two parts — hot and more hot — not to mention a lemon containing liquid fire.)

Colin Dalzell and Bolton Smith concocted a chicken curry served with toasted coconut slivers and tempered with a huge salad, green and cooling. The range of side dishes became ever more varied — some served baked bananas laced with honey and lemon juice, others cut theirs in chunks and rolled them in toasted coconut. Great was the chopping of parsley, the crisping of bacon, the peeling of onions, the grating of hard-boiled eggs, the pulverizing of peanuts, the selection of sweet and sour relishes, the diagnosis of chutnies. And then, as quickly as it had come, the vogue for curry passed, and the

Appleyard Center cooks turned their talents to that challenging item, the Covered Dish.

MENUS FOR CURRY SUPPERS

Twelve-Boy Curry of Lamb Mrs. Appleyard *
Broiled Bananas *
Lemon Sherbet
Oatmeal Cookies ‡
Coffee

The Princess's Curry of Chicken *
Chutney *
Lettuce Salad, French Dressing
Macaroon Trifle *
Tea (Smoky Souchong)

Twelve-Boy Curry of Lamb Mrs. Appleyard

Curry is like tribal lays, concerning which, the poet states, there are a large number of ways of reciting them "and every single one of them is right." Everything about one curry may be a little different from the next, yet both may be excellent. Mrs. Appleyard thinks that on the whole the best curry is made when you meant to all the time and when you are generous with the curry powder. No very distinguished result can be achieved, she says, by suddenly deciding that some uninteresting scraps of meat and some tired gravy would be improved by a dash of curry powder.

This is how she made one that, in the curry cycle, received several kind words.

For six people she took:

A 6-pound shoulder of lamb cut up into slices ¾ inch thick
the lamb bones and trimmings
4 tablespoons butter
4 cups stock (the bones simmered with a carrot, onion, branch of celery)
4 tablespoons flour
4 tablespoons curry powder

2 onions sliced
2 tart apples sliced
1 cup light cream
½ teaspoon cayenne pepper
½ teaspoon pepper from the grinder
salt to taste
extra butter, about 2 tablespoons

She began by simmering the bones and vegetables for 2 hours. This was done the day before she served the curry so that there was time for the fat to rise and be skimmed off.

The next morning she cut the lean meat into cubes, put them into a paper bag with the flour, curry powder and seasonings and tossed them until they were thoroughly coated. Leaving them in a bag for a few minutes she put the butter into her biggest frying pan with the onions and apples, tossed them until they began to soften, then removed them and set them aside. Adding extra butter to the pan, she next gave the pieces of meat a final shaking, put them into the pan and browned them on both sides. She then returned the onion and apple mixture to the pan, scattered in the flour left in the bag, stirring it well into the butter, and added the stock, strained, skimmed and heated.

Mrs. Appleyard then covered the pan, turned the gas low and left the mixture to simmer until the meat was tender, about 2 hours. She looked at it occasionally and added a little hot water. When she was ready to serve it she added the cream. She tasted the sauce at intervals by dipping a piece of bread crust into it. She admits that no useful purpose was served by this gesture because all she did was to say: "Hm, not bad!" but she asserts that if she had felt that it needed more curry she would have added it. No doubt this is so.

She was not idle while the meat was simmering. She was getting the "boys" ready. She has been told — and likes to think that it is so — that in the Orient a different boy carries in each separate relish that accompanies the curry. As this parade is not practical in Vermont, Mrs. Appleyard merely sets out Chinese bowls on trays and lets her guests help themselves.

This lamb curry was a Twelve-Boy Curry and the bowls contained:

Chutney	Peanuts, chopped
Parsley, minced	Yolk of Egg, grated
Spiced Apple Sauce	Green Pepper Relish
White of Egg, chopped	Ginger Marmalade
Tomato Conserve	Fresh Coconut
Onion, chopped fine	Kumquat Preserve

Also served with the curry were broiled bananas and, of course, rice.

When interviewed on the subject of rice Mrs. Appleyard said that she felt too tired to enter into controversy about it at the moment. She merely murmured that when she said "wash it in twelve changes of water" she meant it. Anyone who didn't believe her, she added, was advised to use the quick-cooking kind and do what it said on the package. "Make *plenty!*" she concluded and turned her attention to:

Broiled Bananas

Allow one banana for each person. Slice them lengthwise and cut the slices in halves. Put them cut side up on the tray of the electric grill or in a pan that will fit under your gas broiler. Squeeze lemon juice over the slices, dot them with butter. The broiling takes only a short time — 2 or 3 minutes. Watch them carefully. Bananas should not be green but do not need to be completely ripe.

The Princess's Curry (M.R.)

It was a handsome sight to see the Princess in her white and gold sari bending over the stove in the summer kitchen. If a Baltimore oriole had flown in and started to whip up a chocolate soufflé, Mrs. Appleyard would hardly have been more surprised. However, she preserved her equanimity enough to see how the Princess made the curry.

For eight people she used two broilers, each cut into four pieces and began by browning them carefully in plenty of butter. In the meantime Mrs. Appleyard had chopped three onions and washed brown rice in twelve changes of water. When the chicken had browned, the Princess began to sprinkle curry powder over it, a tablespoon, then another . . . then another . . . then the rest of the bottle. She turned the pieces of chicken carefully, using a spoon and fork, with her sari draped over one arm. Mrs. Appleyard, when she can get some suitable material, changeable red and purple brocaded with silver, perhaps, intends to run up a sari and try this gesture, but hasn't

got round to it yet. At present she is still using a pale blue
smock, a present from Patience Barlow. It's fine for making
cream puffs and oatmeal cookies but she thinks she ought to
have something more sophisticated for curry.

While Mrs. Appleyard was brooding on this subject and
boiling the water for the rice, the Princess began to sprinkle
the chicken with cayenne pepper. She said you should put
in plenty and suited the action to the word. Then she added
the chopped onions and a quart of tomato juice. Mrs. Appleyard made it herself in the blender. The Princess endorsed
this brew and spoke kindly, too, of Mrs. Appleyard's 1955
chutney, so they served some and some crystallized ginger
with the curry.

"Is she," Mrs. Appleyard's youngest granddaughter was
heard to ask Geoffrey Toussaint, "a real princess?"

"Get me half a split pea and we'll put it under her mattress
and find out," answered that gentleman.

Whether the Princess tossed uneasily because of the presence
of the slight lump under the mattress or not, Mrs. Appleyard
is sure she is a real princess.

Chutney

Mrs. Appleyard's ambition has always been to make her
chutney taste like Major Grey's or Colonel Skinner's. She
thinks her 1955 version comes as near as anything to the product endorsed by those revered gentlemen. This is how she
made it. Into her largest preserving kettle she put:

24 tart early apples (Dutchess, Peach, Yellow Transparent, Gravenstein), quartered
8 small onions, chopped
3 large cucumbers, cubed, soaked in brine two hours, drained
4 quarts tomatoes, measured whole, skinned and quartered
1 green pepper, sliced thin
1 4-ounce can pimentos, sliced
3 whole heads of garlic, peeled, sliced
1 pound seeded raisins
1 pound seedless raisins
½ pound currants
3 slices of pineapple, cut fine
3 tablespoons candied ginger, diced
1 cup red wine vinegar
1 cup cider vinegar
2 teaspoons cayenne
3 tablespoons curry powder
2 teaspoons cinnamon
2 pounds brown sugar
2 tablespoons dry mustard
2 teaspoons allspice
6 cups white sugar

Scald the vinegar with the spices and sugar and add it to the mixture of fruits. Bring the contents of the kettle to a boil and cook it for an hour, stirring occasionally. Let it stand overnight. The next morning bring it to a boil again. Better put an asbestos mat under it. It sticks easily at this stage. Cook ½ hour, stirring carefully. Sterilize your jars and rubbers. Remove fruit with a spoon with holes and distribute it in the jars, filling them ⅞ full. Cook the syrup left in the kettle until it is good and thick and fill up the jars with it. About this time it will be safe to invite the neighbors in for curry.

Macaroon Trifle

Mrs. Appleyard, who reads chiefly for the exercise, it is her favorite kind, started in on Thomas Mann's *Buddenbrooks* in German recently. She had read very little German for a number of years. Don't ask us what she was doing instead:

we might tell you and that would be fatiguing for everyone.

At first the language flowed over her without bringing a great deal of meaning with it. Suddenly however there was a succulent description of what the Buddenbrookses had to eat on Christmas Eve. Soon Mrs. Appleyard laid down her book and uttered words with which her family have long been familiar. Like other phrases that have produced a great deal of activity such as "Don't fire till you see the whites of their eyes," "Carthago delenda est," "My kingdom for a horse," the remark was simple and direct.

"I think," said Mrs. Appleyard, "that I could make that."

She did indeed, only why, as a guest who was having his third helping remarked, does she call it a trifle?

You will need, she says, a sponge cake and two dozen macaroons. She does not actually say that you have to make them yourself, so perhaps it would be just as well to start in before she begins to indulge in such fantasies.

1 9-inch sponge cake	1 cup candied fruit (orange
24 macaroons, small	peel, lemon peel, cherries)
1 cup sherry	½ cup blanched almonds
½ cup currant jelly	

Custard:

4 cups scalded milk	½ cup sugar
yolks of 6 eggs	½ teaspoon almond extract
1 teaspoon vanilla	

Make the custard and let it cool while you are arranging the trifle. Beat the eggs slightly with a wire whisk or fork. Add the sugar and beat it in. Pour on the scalded milk, stirring all the time. Cook in a double boiler until the mixture thickens and coats the back of a spoon. This takes about twenty minutes and it cannot be left alone for any length of time but must be stirred pretty constantly. It will curdle if it is left too long, so look out. Add the flavoring. Chill.

Now your handsomest bowl, please. Mrs. Appleyard favors a large one of thousand-eye Sandwich glass which rings when struck like a bell buoy on a foggy day in the Bay of Fundy.

Cut the sponge cake in rather thin slices, spreading each one with the currant jelly, irrigating them slightly with sherry, and sticking the almonds into them as you go along. Arrange a layer of macaroons, sprinkle over some candied fruit and repeat the two layers, first of cake, then of macaroons, till the bowl is full. Macaroons should be on top and will loom up above the custard, which you now pour on, like rocks at low tide. You don't have to do another thing except to chill it for three or four hours and eat it.

Covered-Dish Supper

Most people think of the Fourth of July as the crucial day of that energetic month. Not so Mrs. Appleyard and the Refreshment Committee of the Community Club. In Appleyard Center the Fourth passes almost unnoticed, now that fireworks are forbidden, but as the end of the month approaches, tension mounts. By the last Friday in July barometers are nervously tapped. Thermometers are inspected. Every cloud is assessed to see if it has rain in it. Radios are listened to for rumors of hurricanes, and sufferers from sacroiliac trouble are asked with unusual solicitude whether their backs feel all right. Is it, in short, going to be a good day for the Covered-Dish Supper?

If it is a fine evening — not rainy, not too hot, too windy or too cold — there may be two hundred people to supper on Mrs. Appleyard's lawn. Every casserole will be scraped clean. Cicely Bradshaw and Eleanor Davenport will dash home and make others. Mrs. Appleyard herself may be detected in the twilight snatching materials from her vegetable garden to make extra salads.

Maria Flint's Parker House rolls vanish — all four hundred of them. She hastily bakes a batch of biscuits and sends them over. There isn't a crumb of Marcia Gould's chocolate chiffon cake left, but Cicely finds two angel cakes in her mother's freezer. They were there for an emergency. This is it. When the evening is over and the profits counted, everyone is happily exhausted and there will soon be new shingles on the roof of the Community Club.

If the weather is bad — well, at least, Mrs. Appleyard thinks, everyone who comes has a good time, and you can quite possibly get your casserole back intact and freeze it. For an emergency. People buy the rolls and cakes that are left over. There is plenty of supper left for the workers. They may even get some of Alice Richards' fish casserole.

Organizing this project takes only about the same amount of executive ability as it does to run the General Motors Corporation, so of course everything goes smoothly. Guests and workers take it for granted that coffee will be hot and salads cold. The only person who is surprised by this phenomenon is Mrs. Appleyard. Her burdensome tasks — such as asking Patience Barlow to make corn pudding, and peas and potatoes in cream, getting out the big red tablecloths, arranging flowers in big brown jugs — are over early.

If she tried to do anything else someone is sure to remind her that she has heart trouble. This is a convenient disease, since it can be switched on and off like electricity. Deciding to switch it on, this favorite of fortune relaxes, enjoys the party and marvels at the quiet efficiency of the committee.

Perhaps what she enjoys most is to see the residents of Cranberry Hill — composers, novelists, poets, painters, stage directors — marching in bearing their casseroles. They are all distinguished cooks and it is a dizzy experience to choose among their various masterpieces. It was rumored one summer that they had all chanced on the same cookbook, and another year Martha Carroll was said to have been called on at the last moment to make a substitute casserole for a composer who had let his burn while jotting down a new sonata. But whatever the source the contents are delicious.

The long table is soon loaded with covered dishes: copper, pottery, glass, Swedish iron. There are jellied salads on glass platters and tossed salads in wooden bowls. The best baked beans for miles around — Beth Flint's, Irene Olcott's — are steaming in big enameled pans. Alice Richards' fish casserole has arrived. It's the red one with the blue lining. Mrs. Appleyard just mentions this because someone took the dish home by mistake and Alice wants it back, and no wonder.

There is one table thickly paved with cakes of a toothsome

appearance, being cut into generous squares and triangles by
the committee members' judicial knives. These cakes are as
good as they look. Another table has an enormous coffee per-
colator on it, a silver tower guarding a flock of white cups,
flanked by large white cream pitchers and glass sugar bowls.

All three tables are in the Carriage House, a building that has
been used for many purposes since the carriages were moved
out of it forty years ago. It was a workshop at one time. Later
it was a dormitory for the Appleyard boys and their friends.
When they grew up and went to the wars, Mrs. Appleyard,
tired of seeing the empty beds, turned it into a dance hall for
the next generation. When they in turn grew up and went
away, she installed there the books that she lends: children's
books and her unrivaled collection of mystery stories. Later
she added the materials for whatever handicraft she was learn-
ing by main strength. Highboys six inches tall have been made
here. Pictures have been framed, chairs stenciled, fabrics
painted.

At the moment it is simply a peaceful place to sit and listen
to music, but there are still traces of earlier periods. It has never
been possible to get all the sawdust out of the cracks in the
floor. A sign reading "No Loitering around the Station" is
still nailed to a beam above where Hugh's bed used to stand.
One of his guns, a long rifle a century old, leans up against a
cupboard Stan made. The blue coverlet from his bed is still
lying on the sofa.

Her sons' collection of tall beaver hats still hangs from pegs
on the wall, ready to be snatched off and arrogantly worn by
small boys. There is a great pile of Sally's favorite records.
Stuffed birds, bought at auction by Cicely, who caters to her
mother's weakness for them, look glassily down from the tops

of cabinets. Paint has been worn from the floor by dancing feet. Shoes for a small pony still rest on a wooden bar where they have been for twenty-five years.

Outside on the grass are the Windsor benches borrowed from the church in Gospel Hollow. Seated on these, taking their pleasure with silent solemnity as Vermonters like to do, are people with well-loaded plates. Of course the menu never gives complete satisfaction. There are always some guests who expected "that spoon bread we had last year," or who report that "the man in front of me got the last chunk of pork out of the beans, a real big one. It ought to have been cut smaller."

The complainers are usually men, Mrs. Appleyard notes with interest. There are, of course, a few tigress mothers who feel that their little ones have been slighted.

"Cyril will never *touch* sponge cake," one says with melancholy pride. "Take a piece of the maple butternut, darling, and sit down right over here where we can watch in case anything chocolate is brought in."

"Lilly doesn't have much appetite today," another announces as her child languidly fills her plate for the third time.

Children come for half price and make up for it by eating twice as much as their parents.

Still, on the whole, the customers seem reasonably well pleased. Indeed, one of them, a spry youth of eighty, approaches Mrs. Appleyard and tells her that he spends his time attending church and community suppers throughout the state. He gives this one a good mark, well up toward the top of the list, he says.

"There are good cooks around Sharon, too," he adds; "I'll be down there for a turkey dinner with the Elks next week," and departs with a ghoulish smile.

Tommy Bradshaw has organized his friends into a clean-up squad. They get their supper free in return for their services. Partly out of pride in their work, partly out of interest in what is going to be left when their turn comes, they hover over the guests, ready to snatch plates and cups before they are empty. Mrs. Appleyard prevents, she hopes, several cases of nervous indigestion by feeding the clean-up squad a preliminary sample, about enough for a pride of young lions, and promising them more later.

She wanders into the summer kitchen and succeeds in drying a few coffee cups before she is detected and chased out again.

"Have you had supper? Go out and mingle with your guests," she is told with stern kindness by Cicely.

The guests Mrs. Appleyard really likes best are right here in the kitchen, making coffee, heating rolls, stirring up spaghetti sauce. However, she goes meekly out, joins the queue at the Carriage House, pays her dollar, succeeds in getting some of her own peas and potatoes, Cicely's chef's salad, a piece of her own angel cake.

She thinks it is a pretty sight to see the contributors to the supper helping themselves out of their own covered dishes. There is something rather touching about this preference for the homely familiar over the exotic. It reminds her of the time that Cicely, then four years old, was taken to the bird house at the Zoo. She quietly listened to the screams of macaws and cockatoos; she stared seriously at the toucans and pelicans, then wandered off to look at the parakeets. Suddenly she came running back flushed with excitement.

"Come quick, Mother! Look, in this cage right over here! I've found a *robin!*"

Yet Marion Morris, Cicely's friend from Scotland, had just

jumped as something flew past her showing a breast of orange russet, a back of brownish gray and two white tail feathers and asked: "What is that exotic bird?"

"It's a — a sort of thrush," Mrs. Appleyard said. "We call it a robin."

Marion was a delightful visitor. She liked all sorts of exotic things: robins, baked beans, drive-in movies, supermarkets. She also liked dark green lakes, rocky hilltops and tumbling brooks. They reminded her of Scotland, she said, and added, "You must forgive me for saying that all the time. I can't seem to help it. It must bore you terribly."

"Not at all," said Mrs. Appleyard. "It's very natural. Scotland is the Vermont of Europe, I always say. Do quote me when you get back."

Marion laughed and promised to make this view of Scotland known in the Highland glens.

There is always a high point in any festival. The Appleyard Center Community Supper now reached it with the appearance of two tall white-clad figures. Among the other guests they seemed like visitors from another planet. Margaret Beaufort's beautifully plain white linen suit from Bergdorf Goodman's made flowered prints and peasant skirts something you might see in Woolworth's on a Saturday afternoon. Even Mrs. Appleyard looked apprehensively at her lilac Palm Beach suit, fearing that some enemy might have printed it with petunias. Like every other woman present she wished she had worn different shoes, even if they hurt.

The men, in the face of Barton Beaufort's white linen suit and black bow tie, tried valiantly to improve their appearance. Some tucked in the tails of flannel shirts. Others pulled in their belts. Those who had ties fingered them nervously and tried to pretend that their wives had bought them. They would like to have Barton believe that they wore lightly dressed mermaids and motifs from Picasso's "Guernica" in deference to feminine whim.

Mrs. Appleyard, having invited them, knew that these were not deities from a Greek myth but just the Beauforts. It was true that they wrote Broadway successes with pens mightier than rapiers; yet in Vermont they were delightful neighbors, kind patrons of strawberry festivals, donors of chunks of salmon from the Gaspé, appreciative consumers of such basic simplicities as Quiche Lorraine and Mrs. Appleyard's oatmeal cookies.

Barton had brought a unique contribution to the supper, a box of hand-painted peppermints. He had spent an entire day with vegetable colors and tiny brushes embellishing white mints with four-leaf clovers and maple leaves. There were also suitable Vermont sentiments such as *The Granite Center of the World, More Cows than People* and *Make it Do*.

These peppermint miniatures were such rare works of art that Mrs. Appleyard did not distribute them to the general public but awarded them like medals to the workers. There was a general sentiment that they were too pretty to eat. Perhaps some are still in existence, rapidly becoming pedigreed antiques.

Before long — for even Community Suppers come to an end sometime — the last dish was washed, the last paper cup picked up from the lawn, the last of the coffee drunk (to save it). The Carriage House regained its air of peaceful shabbiness. The trampled grass began to grow again. It was so still that Mrs. Appleyard could hear the brook and the wings of a moth in the larkspur pretending to be a hummingbird. Pink roses were still pink in the glow from the west. The moon came up over East Hill and gilded the white ones.

A blue heron, carefully imitating a Japanese heron painted on silk, flew across the pond and up into the Lady Elm. Mrs.

Appleyard heard an imprudent fish leap and saw the heron fly down and catch it.

I must remember to make more jellied salmon next year, she thought, and slipped serenely into sleep.

ITEMS FROM THE MENU

Fish Casserole (A.R.A.)*
Spaghetti Loaf* with Mushroom Sauce*
Quiche Lorraine*
Jellied Salmon (p. 71)
Baked Beans (I.O.)*
Green Beans Vinaigrette (p. 46)
Green Garden Casserole*

Corn Pudding†
Glazed Beets*
New Potatoes and Peas in Cream (p. 74)
Jellied Salads*
Green Salad (p. 86)
Parker House Rolls (M.F.)*
Cakes: Angel, Sponge, Chiffon,* Layer
Coffee
Souvenir Peppermints

Fish Casserole (A.R.)

3 pounds halibut or any white dry fish (not oily like mackerel)
2 lemons, cut in thin slices

1 cucumber, cut in thin slices
a dozen capers
2 green peppers, cut in thin rounds

In a greased loaf pan lay the ingredients in layers, in this order, fish, dotted with a little butter, lemon, cucumber and pepper slices, a few of the capers. There should be enough for three layers. Pour half a glass of dry white wine over it and bake in a slow oven, 275°, until the fish is tender.

Spaghetti Loaf

½ cup cooked spaghetti
1 cup light cream from the top of the bottle
1 cup bread crumbs, soft part of Pepperidge Farm Bread
¼ cup butter
½ cup sharp cheddar cheese, grated
1 medium onion, minced

2 tablespoons green pepper, chopped
1 pimento, cut into thin slices
3 eggs
1 tablespoon parsley, chopped fine
½ teaspoon thyme, chopped fine
salt to taste

Put butter, crumbs and seasonings in a bowl. Scald the cream and pour it over them. Mix well and stir in the cheese. Add the eggs, well beaten, and the spaghetti. Put the mixture in a well-buttered loaf pan. Dot more butter over the top. Set in a pan of hot water and bake at 350° till firm, about 45 minutes. Turn it out of the pan, slice as you serve it with mushroom sauce.

Mushroom Sauce

Cicely Bradshaw and her mother possess a sort of sixth sense about mushrooms. They think where and when they would grow if they were mushrooms and then go there on the right day and there the mushrooms are. Their shining white caps may gleam like beer cans to the uninitiated but both these mushroom fanciers can spot the difference at 45 m.p.h. They keep their pet fields a secret, even to some extent from each other, and have been known to meet unexpectedly in some upland pasture ten miles from home each equipped with a long sharp knife. So far they have not used these knives for anything more hostile than slicing off the mushroom caps, but who knows what might happen if some outlander intruded upon their privacy.

Actually privacy is difficult when you are picking mushrooms. Mrs. Appleyard and her daughter are not interested in any mushroom except *Agaricus campestris.* This is a fungus of strong character. It will not grow in a piece of ground that is shaded by anything taller than a stalk of white clover. The pasture has to be nibbled down, preferably by horses, and is usually on a sunny slope open to fresh air and city folks.

Yet one year recently these ladies stopped counting when they had frozen, eaten or given away a hundred pounds of mushrooms. They were both out in a well-ventilated pasture last year in the position of the mushroom gatherer — head down, knife in hand — when a large scarlet automobile coasted along the road and eased to a stop.

"Keep your head down," Mrs. Appleyard advised her daughter. "They will think we are peasants — old leech gatherers."

A vibrant male voice from the red car called out: "Hi, Cicely, I knew you by the chopsticks in your hair."

Mrs. Appleyard nominates this simple declarative sentence as one of the most peculiar of the year. Fortunately the owner of the red car is far too busy composing intricate 12-tone jazz to give his attention to mushrooms.

It is a fact that Cicely's dark hair is secured by chopsticks, a style that is spreading so rapidly that she will soon have to initiate something else — old stove lighters perhaps.

In the meantime there is plenty of mushroom sauce in Mrs. Appleyard's freezer, made as follows:

2 pounds mushrooms, caps and tender part of stem only	2 tablespoons flour
1 small onion, minced	salt and pepper to taste
3 tablespoons butter	sherry — if used
	1 cup light cream
pinch of nutmeg	

Wash but do not peel the mushroom caps. Slice the larger ones longitudinally. Leave the button size whole. Fry the onion in the butter till it is straw colored. Add the mushrooms. Cover, and cook till they are tender. Sprinkle the flour and seasonings over them and stir into the butter and juice from the mushrooms which will be in the pan. When thoroughly blended, add the cream, stirring it in slowly, and cook over low heat for 5 minutes. If you like a little sherry in it and are going to use the sauce right away, this is the time to do it — about one tablespoon. If you are going to freeze the sauce do not add the sherry for a couple of years, until you thaw out the package.

Quiche Lorraine

There are probably as many ways of making this as there are cooks. Here is Mrs. Appleyard's version. For six people you will need:

Enough light flaky pastry (p. 93) to line a 10-inch Pyrex pie plate.

1 cup real dairy cheese — New York, Wisconsin, Vermont, coarsely grated.

12 slices of bacon	nutmeg, sugar, cayenne, black
4 eggs	pepper, salt to taste
2 cups light cream	¼ cup chopped chives

Line the pie plate — it should be 1½ inches deep — with your Two-Thousand-Layer paste. Crimp it handsomely around the edges. Prick the bottom lightly with a fork in several places. Put it in the refrigerator for at least 10 minutes. Light the oven — 400°. Fry the bacon until it is crisp but not overcooked. Break it into small pieces and scatter it over the bottom of the pie dish. Sprinkle the chives over this. Beat together the eggs and cream, add the cheese and the seasonings. Bake for 10–15 minutes at 400°. Reduce the temperature to 325° and bake until a silver knife will come out clean from the middle — 25–30 minutes longer. The top should be golden brown, so should the pastry. The bacon and chives will come to the top.

Variations: Finely chopped onions may be substituted for the chives, not more than a teaspoonful.

A little chopped parsley may be sprinkled over the top just before you bring it to the table.

Omit the cheese. Fry a thinly sliced onion golden brown

in the bacon fat. Add a pinch of marjoram and spread the onion over the bacon.

Omit the bacon. Use the cheese and two onions sliced and fried in butter.

Green Garden Casserole

Mrs. Appleyard belongs to the generation that looks with a certain amount of suspicion upon the casserole and not perhaps without justification, for there is no doubt that a casserole can, and does, contain pretty nearly anything. If there are substances you feel strongly about, such as monosodium glutamate and cornstarch — but there, there, calm down, Mrs. Appleyard! Here is one containing none of these things. It hasn't any imitation brick siding or Tiffany glass either. For six people:

1½ cups cold cooked chicken, cubed
2 onions, thinly sliced
½ pound mushrooms, sliced
1 cup cooked spinach
1 cup mushroom stock from stem and peelings
a few spears of chives
1 cup cooked rice

a few sprays of watercress and parsley
2 tablespoons butter
1 cup cooked broccoli
1½ cups sour cream
1 cup chicken stock
1 tablespoon lemon juice
½ cup bread crumbs
an extra tablespoon butter

salt to taste

Sauté the onions in 2 tablespoons of butter until they are pale yellow. Add the mushrooms and cook slowly till they are tender. Put the cooked spinach, mushroom and chicken stocks, sour cream, watercress, parsley, chives, lemon juice into the electric blender. Run it until everything is smoothly blended, about a minute. Pour this green mixture over the mushrooms and onions, add the chicken, the broccoli and the rice. Put it into your best Dutch iron casserole, sprinkle with bread crumbs, dot with butter. Bake at 375° until the top is well browned — 15–20 minutes.

Baked Beans (I.G.O.)

Soak 8 cups of soldier beans for several hours, although beans do not need so much soaking these days as formerly, and it is not necessary to do it overnight. Parboil them. Take your bean pot and put in 1 pound salt pork in chunks, 1 pound brown sugar, an onion, quartered, some dry mustard, salt and pepper. Bake in a slow oven, covered, until they are done. Don't let them dry out. This is as near as a good cook can get to telling you how she makes beans fit for a queen. Soldier beans have a little soldier down one seam. Around Appleyard Center they are preferred to all others for baking, far above pea beans, red kidney beans or yellow-eyes. A few people use maple syrup in place of brown sugar. For a big supper they are often baked in a wide enamel dishpan, round or oval, so they can be heated up easily and served readily at the table. No covered-dish supper would be complete without them.

Glazed Beets

Use beets that are young and tender. One of the great advantages in doing so is that then you are not confronted with them when they are old and tough. Some long winter evening when the loud howling of the wolves is heard between the icicles, Mrs. Appleyard will tell how she and Venetia Hopkins made beet wine. But not tonight.

Cook the beets in plenty of water. Slip them out of their skins, slice them and set them where they will keep warm. There should be about two cups. Cook the beet juice down until you have one cup. Soak 1 tablespoon minute tapioca in ¼ cup beet juice for 5 minutes. Add 2 tablespoons lemon juice, 2 tablespoons red wine, salt and pepper to taste. Stir this mixture into the cup of beet juice. Cook till it starts to thicken. Add the sliced beets. Serve as soon as they are hot, with the sauce poured over them.

Jellied Salads

SHRIMP AND COLE SLAW

1 package Lemon or Lime Jello
1 cup mayonnaise
1 cup finely shredded cabbage
1 cup finely shredded carrot
1 cup small cleaned shrimp
½ cup crushed pineapple

Prepare the Jello according to the directions on the package. When it is partly chilled stir in the mayonnaise, cabbage, carrot and pineapple. Rinse a ring mold with cold water or brush with oil. Put in one quarter of the mixture. Distribute the shrimp around the ring. Fill with the remaining mixture. Chill, turn out of the mold, and arrange on platter with leaf lettuce.

GRAPE JUICE AND FRUIT

1 package Grape Jello
3 cups fruit cocktail or the equivalent in fresh cut-up fruit except fresh pineapple

½ cup walnuts, chopped
1 can concentrated grape juice

Prepare the Grape Jello according to the directions on the package, substituting the concentrated grape juice for part of the required liquid. When partly chilled stir in the fruit and nuts. Place in fancy mold, complete chilling and unmold on glass platter. Serve with mayonnaise into which ½ cup whipped cream has been stirred, also a little sugar.

Parker House Rolls (M.F.)

For 2½ dozen — Time 15 minutes, oven at 400°
3¼ cups bread flour (Occident) sifted

1⅓ cups milk
1 cake yeast
3 tablespoons sugar
1 teaspoon salt
3 tablespoons shortening

Scald milk and cool until lukewarm. Dissolve yeast and sugar in ⅓ cup of warm milk. Sift flour before and after measuring. Combine dissolved yeast and sugar and salt with the remainder of the milk. Add one half the flour and beat thoroughly. Add melted shortening. Add remainder of flour gradually and beat thoroughly after each addition. Turn onto lightly floured board and knead until smooth and elastic. Place in bowl and cover and allow to rise in warm place, 80°–85°, until double in bulk, about 1½ hours. Punch down and let rise again.

Shape into rolls, rolling the dough to ¼ inch thickness. Cut with biscuit cutter. Crease through center. Spread one half with thin layer of butter. Fold one half well over the other half. Place about ½ inch apart on greased baking sheet. Allow to rise until very light, about 45 minutes. Bake in moderate oven.

Orange Chiffon Cake (M.G.)

Sift together in one bowl:

2¼ cups Softasilk or 2 cups Gold Medal flour

1½ cups sugar

3 teaspoons double acting baking powder

1 teaspoon salt

Make a well in the center and in it put:

½ cup salad oil
¾ cup cold water
flavoring — 2 teaspoons vanilla
    or 2 teaspoons almond or 2
    teaspoons lemon rind

Mix well. Set your oven at 325° for a 10-inch tube pan, or at 350° for a 9 x 13 pan. Beat 1 cup egg whites in a large bowl with ½ teaspoon cream of tartar until very dry and stiff. Fold the yolk mixture very gently into the whites. Pour into ungreased tube or oblong pan. Bake the tube cake for about an hour at 325°, the oblong one at 350° for 45–50 minutes, or until the top springs back when pressed.

Slice a cake made in the tube pan in three horizontal layers and fill with the following:

Rich Orange Filling

In a saucepan put:

1 cup sugar
4 tablespoons cornstarch
½ teaspoon salt
1 cup orange juice
2 teaspoons orange rind — optional

1½ teaspoons lemon juice
2 tablespoons butter
(orange juice frozen concentrate can be used in place of juice and sugar)

Bring to a rolling boil and boil 1 minute, stirring constantly. Chill well before using.

Frost the cake with a 7-minute boiled icing and decorate with some of the orange filling spooned over the top. This is a delicate cake and should be served right after it is baked.

Chocolate Icing (M.L.G.)

For a vanilla- or almond-flavored chiffon cake use the following icing:

Melt together 4 tablespoons butter and 4 squares chocolate. Blend in 2⅔ cups sifted confectioners' sugar and ⅓ teaspoon salt. Add 6½ tablespoons heated milk and 1¼ teaspoons vanilla. Beat till smooth and glossy.

August

A Bounty of Beans

M RS. APPLEYARD in a burst of shallow optimism picked
up the telephone with the idea of making a call to Cicely.
She wished to discuss some Henry James characters with whom
she and her daughter were currently involved. She forgot that it
is easier to call Paris from a pay station than it is to get East
Alcott from an eight-party line. There was as usual a deceptive
silence during which she hoped to hear the languid voice of the
operator, in case she was not out having a cup of instant coffee.

What's instant about it? Mrs. Appleyard wondered. Certainly
not the consumption time.

Then she heard The Sigh and realized that she was listening to a conversation. The Sigh is a standard part of an eight-party line causerie. It follows a silence and precedes a statement. In this case the statement was: "My beans have come on awful sudden."

Mrs. Appleyard put down the receiver in dismay, for well she knew that when one bean ripens, all ripen. Every year she studies the seed catalogue with the idea of growing beans so that they will be ready at convenient intervals. The beans in the catalogue know how to accomplish this. They are literate, educated beans. They ripen in sixty-three days, in sixty-eight, in seventy-two. You can plant all the kinds the same day and count on a two-week span of perfect green pods, tender and delicious.

That must happen in some effete southern state such as Massachusetts. Transported to the rugged air of Vermont, threatened by late frosts in June and early frosts in August, scorched by July suns, soaked by cloudbursts, beans pay no attention to what it says on the package. They know they must achieve their destiny before it is too late. They keep right on growing by moonlight if necessary, by fireflyshine or aurora borealis. There is no use planting them at different intervals either. They know better than you do when they are ready for the freezer.

Beans must be dealt with like small children in a tantrum — kindly, firmly and at once. You must eat them, freeze them or give them away. The last is the hardest because practically everyone else is in the same dilemma. However, there are always a few people who are strong-minded enough not to have gardens. No doubt these hardy targets for horticultural benevolence privately throw away a good many vegetable donations, but this must be considered their own affair.

Never question the contents of your neighbor's compost heap or casserole. (Quoted by permission from *Mrs. Appleyard's Condensed Wisdom*, p. 398.)

Having frozen enough beans in their time to make, if carefully packaged, piled and frozen, enough igloos for an Eskimo supermarket, Mrs. Appleyard and Patience have developed what they regard as a good box of beans.

Boil the beans ten minutes, Mrs. Appleyard says. It is not necessary to cook all the water away. Pour it right into the package with the beans. It will help to keep them from drying out. When you finish cooking them — next year, two years from now — it will serve as the water in which you cook them. You need then put only a quarter of a cup of boiling water into your saucepan, just to start the thawing process as quickly as possible.

To get back to getting beans ready for the freezer: when your ten minutes are up, have a large pan of cold water ready and set your pan of hot beans into it to cool for five minutes. Then put the beans into the package, label and date it and into the freezer with it. Remember to set your freezer at sharp freeze before you start on one of these bean-freezing orgies. If it is at its coldest setting and if you put in only one package at a time, a good many can be safely frozen during the course of a day, about all you will be able to cut, probably. Keep the freezer set at sharp freeze for the next few days because you are going to be busy with that knife. At the end of that time you will never wish to see another bean, but by Thanksgiving time you will feel differently.

When you start cooking your beans for the Thanksgiving dinner, put a quarter cup of water into a saucepan. When it boils add the beans. Cover. After four minutes uncover and add butter. They should finish cooking in about three minutes more. The water will have cooked out; the beans will be crisp and tender. Never put soda in beans. All right, it does make them green but it also kills the vitamins and the flavor.

Mrs. Appleyard and Patience do peas by substantially the same method. They pick only enough for one or two packages at a time, shell only enough for one package, cook them in just enough water to cover them for about four minutes, package them in the water in which they are cooked, and freeze them as you do the beans. When serving them Mrs. Appleyard starts them cooking in two tablespoonfuls of boiling water. They need only two or three minutes cooking after they start to boil. Add butter the last minute. It speeds up the cooking process. This applies to the beans too.

It is almost impossible to tell these peas from peas actually fresh from the garden. That is assuming that they were young and tender when you picked and cooked them, and that Patience has marked them A plus. Mrs. Appleyard has said this before but she repeats it here because it is a fact often forgotten: you are not going to get anything out of the freezer better than what you put into it.

These frozen peas are so precious that she never serves them except perfectly plain with butter and possibly a very little thick cream. Beans however are more plentiful by far, and she has several different ways of serving them: beans with mushrooms, beans with croutons, beans and potatoes with onions, cream and beef cracklings, wreath of beans around a cauliflower, with Hollandaise sauce, beans with cream, sprinkled with parsley and crisp crumbled bacon.

Let the beans come on!

You might just as well, Mrs. Appleyard says, accept this simultaneity of beans as you accept the Precession of the Equinoxes, get out your sharpest knife and go to work. Whether the resulting packages will contain a reasonable facsimile of beans or whether they will shelter chunks of brownish-green blotting paper will depend a good deal on how you cut them. You might just as well, she says, leave them on the vines as break them into pieces and throw them into brine.

This is the method worked out by Patience Barlow, who not only dominates the bean freezing session (Mrs. Appleyard is just an extra pair of hands) but who conscientiously labels the packages with grades ranging from B to A plus. They begin by cutting the beans as thin as possible on a long diagonal. This may be done with scissors or with a gadget designed for the purpose. Mrs. Appleyard prefers a French vegetable knife and a cutting board. Patience deftly whittles them in the air with a skill all her own.

They do only enough for a package at a time, add them to a pan containing only just enough boiling water to cover them. No salt. It only toughens and discolors them. It can be added just before they are sent to the table months later.

Menus for Dinners in Green Bean Season

Hot Clear Beet Soup*   Toasted Montpelier Crackers
Roast Beef*   Yorkshire Pudding (p. 221)
Roasted Potatoes in the Pan
Cauliflower and Green Beans Hollandaise *
Peach Short Cake
Coffee

Clear Mushroom Broth   Melba Toast
Roast Lamb *   Roasted Potatoes in the Pan *
Currant Jelly

Green Beans with Sour Cream Sauce*
Deep Dish Apple Pie   Hard Sauce

Hot Spcied Tomato Juice (p. 16)
Cheese and Chutney Appetizers
Stuffed Mushroom Caps *
Smothered Veal*
Green Beans with Cream Beef Cracklings *
Corn, 20 minutes from Garden to Table
Chocolate Icebox Cake*

Hot Clear Beet Soup

4 cups clear beet juice	1 onion, sliced thin
1 can consommé	2 tablespoons instant tapioca
	2 tablespoons sherry

Combine the beet juice and the consommé. Mrs. Appleyard hopes you saved the juice when you cooked your last batch of beets for vegetable salad. If you did not, you have her permission to be extravagant and pour it off cans of beets until you have enough. What you do with the beets is your problem. Slice the onion very thin and pour the beet juice and consommé over it. Do this an hour before dinner. Soak the tapioca in some of the beet juice. When you are ready to serve the soup, strain out the onion, add the tapioca and cook gently for three minutes. Add the sherry. Serve with sliced lemon in the plate and pass sour cream with it.

Roast Beef

It was recently called to Mrs. Appleyard's attention that she has never told a hungry world how to roast beef. The truth is she supposed that everyone knew how. Until people began to ask her, she had forgotten that a whole generation of housewives had grown up who had never been exposed to anything more exacting than a pound of hamburg.

During that period Mrs. Appleyard, always ready to try anything new, has experimented with the constant-temperature method and has now gone back to searing a roast and basting it. However, as a concession to modernity she uses a meat thermometer. If you have ten or twelve dollars worth of beef in the oven it helps your morale considerably to be able to read a device that tells you when it is done. She also uses one of those basters that looks like a giant medicine dropper. This is also a great help. However, there is no method that will free you completely from responsibility. You still must calculate the approximate time of cooking before you ever put the beef into the oven so that you will know when to cook the rest of the dinner. Be sure you know accurately what the roast weighs.

For roasts with the bone in, allow:
For rare: 13–15 minutes to the pound
For well done: 18–20 minutes to the pound
For roasts without bones allow:
For rare: 15–18 minutes to the pound
For well done: 20–22 minutes to the pound

Begin with the oven at 450°. Rub flour all over the roast and well into it. Insert the thermometer. Don't let it touch the bone. Put the meat into a large roasting pan big enough to hold the roast comfortably and leave room for the potatoes. Do not cover the pan. Dredge more flour over the beef, letting some fall into the pan. When this begins to brown, as it will do in about 20 minutes, reduce the heat to 300° and start basting.

Mrs. Appleyard likes for basting some hot broth made by simmering beef bones with a carrot, an onion, a branch of celery, a few herbs, a dash of cinnamon, a pinch of nutmeg, but plain water sometimes has to do. The gravy, in case you make it, will not be quite so good but the flavor of the meat will not be changed to any extent. She likes the gravy that runs out of the meat best herself and so, she notices, do a great many other people. Anyway, for the first few bastings — do it every 15 minutes — you will need to add some liquid to the pan and it should be hot. When the fat begins to run into the pan, it will not be necessary to add any more liquid until you make the gravy. When you do, use some more of the hot stock. If Mrs. Appleyard said what she thinks about gravy makers and monosodium glutamate and so-called bouillon cubes, this book would not be allowed to go through the mails. She forbears.

When the thermometer reads just exactly what you wish it to say, take the pan out of the oven *at once*. Remember that the meat, especially if there are bones acting as heat conductors in it, will go on cooking inside after you have taken it out of the oven. If your guests are a little late it is better to take it out ahead of time, cover it, let it stand until you are ready to serve it, then return it to the oven for a few minutes.

By this method the fat will be brown and crisp. There will be some well done slices for those who like it that way. The inside will be tender and juicy. There will be plenty of dish gravy.

Perhaps the most valuable piece of advice Mrs. Appleyard can give you is about carving: never let a man less than sixty years old do it unless he has a diploma from a certified carving school embossed on his shirt front. Youth is a wonderful thing but an ability to carve is not one of its attributes. Mrs. Appleyard thinks carving should be done by men — a strong, just and generous sex — but it is an art and they should study it. Cutting up frankfurters for the nursery school set and serving casseroles are not suitable preparation for this task. Your husband needs a good book and something to practice on before he carves in public. He also needs a well-tempered steel knife and the ability to make and keep it sharp.

Roast Potatoes around the Meat

Parboil potatoes in their skins for twenty minutes. Run cold water over them. Peel them. Cut them in halves. Melt some beef fat — you are supposed to save it and have a jar in the refrigerator — or some butter in a frying pan. Turn the potatoes over in this until they are buttered all over. Put them into the pan with the beef. Baste them when you baste the beef. Turn them occasionally so they will brown evenly. This takes about 45 or 50 minutes, depending on the size. They should be crisp and brown outside and fluffy inside.

Cauliflower and Green Beans Hollandaise

This is simply a perfect head of cauliflower, cooked until it is just done but will still hold its shape (Mrs. Appleyard cooks hers in a steamer) and surrounded by a garland of green beans thinly sliced. The beans are dotted here and there with tiny croutons carefully browned and crisped in butter. The cauliflower is covered with Hollandaise sauce. Since the cauliflower takes longer than the beans, start it first. And since the Hollandaise is difficult to keep hot without curdling, make it last. Mrs. Appleyard has printed the rule for this so many times (in *Mrs. Appleyard's Kitchen* to mention one place) that she will not repeat it here.

Roast Lamb

Mrs. Appleyard uses the same method for roast lamb as for beef. (See p. 131). Because of the difficulty of procuring skilful carvers — she is definitely not one herself — she usually has the lamb boned. She brings home the bones and trimmings and makes broth for basting from them. For some reason more people seem to like brown gravy with lamb than with beef, so she usually makes it, as soon as the meat and potatoes are on her big well-and-tree platter. First she browns some flour in a frying pan, working it into the flour and fat already in the pan. Then she pours on some of the hot broth, blends it well, lets it cook a minute or two, strains it into the gravy boat.

For lamb that is to be just pink in the middle she allows 18 minutes with the bone in; without the bone 20 minutes to the pound. If it is to be well done she allows 22 minutes to the pound. These are approximations for guidance in timing the whole meal. The thermometer will give the final and correct answer.

Green Beans with Sour Cream Sauce

Mrs. Appleyard thinks wistfully of the time when you got sour cream by skimming it off ten quarts of milk which was standing around in the back buttery. However, modern soured cream is more generally available than that butter-colored stuff that comes off the pans with the scarlet edges. It's good too.

Here's a sauce that goes well with poached salmon, with fish mousse or with asparagus, or green beans, as in this case.

Sour Cream Sauce

3 egg yolks
½ tablespoon vinegar
what seasonings you like — salt, pepper, paprika
1 cup sour cream
½ tablespoon lemon juice

Put the vinegar and lemon juice into the top of a double boiler, beat in the egg yolks, then the cream, a third at a time. Remove at once from the heat and serve with green beans.

Cheese and Chutney Appetizers

rounds of bread toasted on one side
¼ pound butter
½ pound dairy cheese, grated
½ cup Mrs. Appleyard's Chutney (p. 103)
1 tablespoon finely minced onion
a little Worcestershire sauce if you like it

Butter the bread on the toasted side. Mix the rest of the ingredients and spread the rounds of bread with the mixture. Put them on a baking sheet and bake them at 375° until the cheese melts — about five minutes.

Stuffed Mushroom Caps

Raw mushroom caps, mouthful size, filled with cream cheese, thick cream, chopped chives and minced parsley and dusted over with paprika.

Smothered Veal (For 6) (V.H.)

2 pounds of veal, cut from the leg in inch-thick slices and cut into neat pieces, 2 x 3 inches. (Save the trimmings for Veal and Ham Pie or Pâté)

1 cup flour seasoned with pepper, salt, a little oregano, marjoram, rosemary — or what you like

4 cups hot water

2 good-sized onions, finely sliced

2 tablespoons butter

1 cup thin cream or top of the bottle

2 tablespoons white wine

2 tablespoons minced parsley

2 tablespoons chopped chives

Fry the onions in the butter until they are light yellow. While they are cooking put the seasoned flour in a bag and shake the pieces of veal in it until they are well coated. Remove the onions temporarily from the pan and brown the veal until it is crisp on both sides. Put the onions back with the veal, pour the hot water over and let it simmer over a very low flame until

it is tender — about an hour. Longer will do no harm but replace the water occasionally. It should not cook dry. When
it is tender, add the cream and let it cook a minute. Then stir in
the wine. Mrs. Appleyard uses her biggest scarlet and ivory
frying pan for this and brings it to the table right in the pan
with the parsley and chives sprinkled over the top.

Green Beans with Cream and Beef Cracklings

Prepare the cracklings beforehand (p. 75). Slice the beans
on the long diagonal. Cook them in rapidly boiling water, not
too much of it, and when it has cooked away, add a little very
thick cream. Before serving them heat the cracklings briefly,
skim them out of the pan, using a spoon with holes so you will
not get any fat with them and sprinkle them over the beans.

Chocolate Icebox Cake (P.K.)

One of the nice things about giving Kitchen Privileges, Mrs.
Appleyard says, is that someone is always making something in
your kitchen. You may, for instance, open your refrigerator
and find a Pyrex loaf pan in it lined with waxed paper with the
paper neatly folded over the top. The contents are a mystery
and remain so until Phyllis unveils her mother's Chocolate Icebox Cake.

¾ pound chocolate bits	6 large (or 7 small) eggs
4½ tablespoons hot water	1 teaspoon vanilla
3 tablespoons powdered sugar	1½ dozen lady fingers
½ pint cream, whipped	

Melt the chocolate bits over hot water with the hot water and sugar. Add the egg yolks lightly beaten and cook over hot water until the mixture thickens and coats the back of the spoon. It takes about seven minutes. Remove from the fire and let it cool while you beat the whites stiff but not dry. Add the vanilla. Fold in the whites.

Line a Pyrex loaf pan with wax paper, leaving enough at the ends and sides to fold over the top. Line the pan, bottom, sides and ends with lady fingers. Put in half the chocolate mixture; lay some more lady fingers on top of it. Add the rest of the chocolate and finish with lady fingers. Fold over the paper. Put the pan in the refrigerator for at least 4 hours. When you serve it turn the loaf out of the pan and frost it with whipped cream. Deadly, but *good!*

Gourmets on Safari

FROM THE BEGINNING Cicely was a puzzle to the Beauforts. Presumably well educated, since she had been to Bryn Mawr, fond of reading to the point of vice, why was she not also well informed? Her refusal to read the *New York Times* every day, like other normal people, quite shocked them. It was not until the expedition to Catamount Brook that they finally found a satisfactory classification for her.

Cicely, they told Venetia Hopkins, at whose house they had been staying, was a Shakespearean nature sprite.

Just what this meant Cicely was never quite sure, but it clearly made the Beauforts happy to have found a pigeonhole for her. Nature sprites obviously had little time for newspaper reading. They were more in the line of inspectors of sunrises, guardians of lady-slippers, cherishers of semi-precious stones.

The Beauforts were fond of picnics and when Cicely volunteered to conduct them up Catamount Brook to a certain series of pools they accepted agreeably. The date was set and at the last moment a family of friends from New Hampshire who were calling on the Beauforts joined the party. The Daltons were advertised as hearty lovers of the outdoors, but their reaction to Catamount Brook confirmed Cicely's private conviction that New Hampshire is a rather decadent state.

It had been decreed by the Beauforts, and accepted by Cicely, that there were to be no paper plates and cups on this picnic. The Beauforts lived with an elegance so thoroughgoing that one could not imagine them using anything made of plastic, let alone paper. Thus a complete service for twelve in silver and crystal was to be transported up the mountainside, along with the various items on the menu. Barton Beaufort made himself responsible for the wine.

The departure of the picnickers from Appleyard Center was uneventful, except that Cicely forgot the large pan of Gazpacho over which she had been working for two days and had to go back three miles to get it. She found the party gathered at the foot of the trail. As Barton had brought along the Sunday edition of the *New York Times* no one lacked for reading matter, and the children were picking flowers in the overgrown hayfield.

The first part of the climb offered no special problems, although some of the cartons, containers and baskets in which the meal was packed had to be redistributed several times along the way. It was not until they reached the point where it is necessary to leave the trail and descend Catamount Brook itself that difficulties began to arise.

The mountain range of which Catamount is the northernmost peak is made of a mica-laden metamorphic rock. Rough garnets can be found in the upper ledges. The brooks that leap down its sides are icy, green in their pools, white and rushing in their more level stretches. Spring freshets have tumbled boulders of all sizes down their courses, along with uprooted trees and smaller driftwood. It is not, to say the least, easy going on Catamount Brook.

The Bradshaw children, born and bred in this briar patch, leapt like chamois from rock to rock, except for Camilla, who rode alternately on her mother's back or on her hip. But the Dalton children cowered and whimpered at the top of each ledge and had to be lowered from adult to adult along with the provisions, the cutlery, the napery and the wineglasses.

When Cicely came to the goal of the picnic, a deep emerald pool fifteen feet long with a sandbar at the lower end where they could all comfortably sit and eat, she plunged in and swam its full length. Perhaps it was this gesture as much as anything which pinned the nature sprite label on her. No one followed her example. One of the Dalton children was crying now and its mother did not know whether to comfort it or drown it.

Finally all the animate and inanimate essentials were assembled on the sandbar. Barton set the bottles of Liebfraumilch to cool in the brook and began carving the ham in delicate slices. Cicely ladled the Gazpacho into brown pottery bowls. There was French bread and butter and the children were allowed to make sandwiches if they wished.

For dessert an angel cake came out of its pan and a pot-pourri of fruit in red wine — peaches, canteloupe, white grapes, raspberries, orange sections, flavored with mint from Cicely's garden — from a Thermos container. The Liebfraumilch was served throughout the meal in appropriate glasses. Slowly the capacity of food and drink to soothe and calm exerted its customary spell. Even Mr. Dalton regained a measure of peace of mind after his ordeal — it was he who halfway down the brook had refused to go any farther, saying he had never liked the outdoors anyway. Barton had to coax him down the last ledge with a glass of Liebfraumilch.

The way home was reasonably easy, though occasionally a marshy trickle had to be forded. Only one of Venetia's wine glasses had slipped into the pool and could not be retrieved, though Tommy Bradshaw tried diving for it. The water was so clear that they could see it, deceptively within reach.

"An unusual form of libation," said Barton, emptying the last of the wine bottles into the pool. "I doubt if they often get the glass too."

Cicely felt that Englishmen who dressed for dinner on desert islands had nothing on the Beauforts.

Mountain Menus

Gazpacho *
Ham — Harrington's Cob-smoked
French Bread   Sweet Butter
Angel Cake
Pot-pourri of Fruit in Red Wine *
Liebfraumilch
Cornish Pastries *

Salad in the Hand — carrot sticks, hearts of celery,
  radishes, raw broccoli, raw cauliflower — blue
  cheese dip
Tomato Juice
Green Ripe Olives
Apricot-Nut Bars *

Gazpacho

4 tablespoons mixed chopped
  fresh herbs, such as parsley,
  dill, chives, basil, marjoram,
  savory
6 large ripe tomatoes, skinned
  and chopped

2 cloves of garlic, chopped fine
  or pressed
2 big sweet peppers, quartered
  and chopped fine

With a potato masher crush the whole mixture and add
gradually juice of 2 lemons and 1 cup olive oil, until the mixture
is a paste. Stir in 6 cups homemade chicken stock. Season to
taste with salt and ground black pepper. Add 2 cups cucumbers,
peeled, seeded and chopped fine, also 1 Bermuda onion and 2
hearts of celery, chopped fine likewise. Chill 4 hours before
serving. Serves six.

Pot-pourri of Fruit in Red Wine

Cut up 4 fresh peaches, 1 canteloupe. Add one package
frozen raspberries, one package frozen strawberries, one large
can orange juice — frozen concentrate, 1 cup seedless grapes.
Add ½ cup honey, 2 tablespoons finely chopped mint leaves,

½ teaspoon mint extract, 2 cups dry red wine. Stir together and chill. Prepare at least 2 hours before serving. Serves six to 8.

Cornish Pasties

Prepare enough pastry for a two-layer pie — this will make six good-sized pasties. Roll out and cut 6-inch circles. Chop 1 pound good stewing beef — chuck or bottom round — into small cubes, ½-inch square. Include some fat. Chop coarsely 3 carrots, 2 medium onions, a little turnip if you like it, and 3 medium potatoes. Mix the meat and vegetables in a bowl, salt and pepper them lightly. Put some of the mixture on half of each circle. Dot with butter. Be generous but leave an edge; fold the other half of the circle over and pinch it well together. Prick holes in the top. Place on baking sheet and bake at 400° until done. The pasties will be browned top and bottom. It will take about an hour. Reduce the heat the last third of the baking time. Cool the pasties and eat them cold in the hand.

Apricot-Nut Bars

½ cup flour	1 cup light brown sugar
½ teaspoon salt	½ cup almonds, chopped
1 teaspoon baking powder	1 cup chopped apricots
2 eggs	1 teaspoon almond extract

Stir together flour, salt and baking powder. Beat the eggs; beat in the sugar gradually; stir in the nuts, apricots and almond extract; stir in the dry ingredients. Spread in 8 x 8 pan well greased. Bake in moderate oven — 350° — about 30 minutes or until surface springs back. Cut at once into squares and roll in powdered sugar. Makes 16.

The Corn is Yellow

F ROM ONE POINT of view the year 1955 was a grim one. This was the year the crows pulled up all Mrs. Appleyard's corn. They were not particular about varieties: Golden Bantam, Midget Marvel, Gold Cross, Sugar and Gold, all were acceptable to their shiny beaks. Roger Willard planted the corn again. The next week a spring freshet, mistaking the vegetable garden for a river bed, washed most of the corn seed down into the witch grass at the bottom of the slope. It was replanted. What corn came up reared its head just in time to be met by a frost.

Naturally under such conditions ingenuity was necessary if Mrs. Appleyard was going to carry on the proud tradition left to her to maintain by generations of her husband's ancestors: that in August you eat corn. She was subjected to the indignity of buying corn, thus putting a blot upon her bright escutcheon, for it was an old Appleyard maxim that corn is not fit to eat unless it reaches the kettle no more than twenty minutes after it is picked. However, there are ways to serve it besides on the cob with plenty of butter, ways in which the elusive sweet freshness of the corn would be obscured anyway by other flavors.

It was rather relaxing not to have to start freezing corn as soon as the last bean was in its neat blue and white checked package. There is no use, Mrs. Appleyard says, in freezing it except from your own garden: you might as well save your energy and buy Golden Bantam next winter in a can.

Saved-up energy is something like the daylight you save every summer, or like champagne at the bottom of the bottle. Unless it is used at once the fizz goes out of it.

"Are you in a mood to experiment?" Mrs. Appleyard inquired of Patience Barlow.

Patience guessed she was. What else could she say? She looked slightly apprehensive, however. She was thinking perhaps of the time Mrs. Appleyard decreed that they would have something to eat every day for a week that they had never cooked before. That was the week they had Crêpes Suzette, Lobster Thermidor, Lady Baltimore Cake, Roast Lamb with anchovies, parsley and watercress, Shoofly Pie, Vol-au-Vent of Sweetbreads with mushrooms. That was all: just six items. There are, to be sure, seven days in a week. On the seventh day both ladies ate milk toast — not just ordinary milk toast with ordinary Jersey milk, mostly cream — with skimmed milk.

Mrs. Appleyard's daughter Sally Roland drove over from Roland Hill and found her mother flanked by handwritten cookbooks, busily making notes and murmuring a sort of tribal incantation containing such terms as Aunt Anne's Corn Fritters, Cousin Charlotte's Corn Pudding, Grandmother's Chowder,

Seraphina's Pancakes . . . casserole . . . omelet . . . Amanda's Smothered Chicken.

"This should be set to music," Sally suggested, for August is not only the corn season in Appleyard Center. It is also the season when the Music School makes Roland Hill resonant. Roland Hill once had an Institute of Arts and Letters, but after a while it was decided that one type of genius was enough. Mrs. Appleyard has a strange untutored liking for music and a great affection for mus'cians. She says that if the different nationalities in the United Nations co-operated the way musicians from different nations do in a symphony orchestra, all our political problems would be solved. Suppose the first cellist doesn't like the second flute. He doesn't play out of tune just to spite him.

Sally said she understood that not all musicians were devoid of egotism.

"Robin Viereck told me a story about two old fiddlers," she said. "One of them said to the other: 'Bill, you tune your A a little mite sharper than mine. Then they'll know there's two of us playing.'"

"That," said her mother, "was just an honest Vermont way of being sure that the customers knew they were getting their money's worth. Only probably most of them were like me and wouldn't know the difference. Patience, I think that chicken needs smothering, and if there's any left we'll make Seraphina's casserole tomorrow. Sally, you'd better come over this evening and bring some people to sing rounds. Cicely's coming, with Alice Richards and Eleanor Davenport and the Hiltons. Read this rule of your Great-aunt Amanda's. Doesn't it sound good?"

Sally read it and announced that she saw only two defects in it. There wouldn't be any left for a casserole and no one could possibly sing after they had eaten it.

"They can sing out of tune," her mother said placidly. "Then we'll know they're all trying."

Menus

Supper for Singers

Smothered Chicken with Corn *
Green Beans with Croutons and Crisp Bacon
Cheese Biscuits
Soufflé in a Double Boiler *
Foamy Sauce *

Supper for the Family on a Cool Evening

Vermont Cheese Soup with Corn *
Graham Sour Milk Bread *
Peach Upside Down Cake, Vanilla Ice Cream

Dinner for Mountain Climbers Who Had Sandwiches for Lunch

Chicken Pie
Glazed Carrots *
Succotash — Shell Beans and Corn
Lettuce Salad
Raspberries with Cream
Brownies

Smothered Chicken with Corn

For eight:

2 broilers cut into 8 pieces, wing tips off
4 tablespoons chicken fat
2 cups chicken stock (make this the day before)

corn cut from 6 large ears of Golden Bantam
minced parsley
2 tablespoons butter

Put the flour, seasoned as you like it, into a bag. Put in the pieces of chicken and toss them until they are thoroughly floured. Melt the chicken fat and the butter in a large frying pan and cook the pieces of chicken in it, 5 minutes on a side. Add the chicken stock. (Mrs. Appleyard makes it from the neck and wing tips simmered with carrot, onion and celery. She adds any stock left over from boiling fowls. A package or two of this in the freezer is handy to have, she says). Cover the pan and let the chicken cook half an hour longer on very low heat. Turn the heat up, add more stock or water if necessary. Put in the cut corn, and cook till the corn is done, about 15 minutes. Sprinkle with the minced parsley and serve.

Soufflé in a Double Boiler

This is a little less strain on the nerves than an oven-baked soufflé as it can be left for a short time over hot (not boiling) water to keep warm if necessary.

4 egg whites
3 tablespoons orange marmalade
(or 3 tablespoons sweetened

apricot pulp, grated rind 1
lemon)
4 tablespoons sugar
grated rind 1 orange

Beat the egg whites until they make stiff peaks but are not dry. Mix sugar, marmalade and rind well together and fold gently into the egg whites. Butter the top of a double boiler. Put in the mixture, cover, and cook for one hour over water that is just boiling.

In the meantime make Foamy Sauce, using the egg yolks. When the time comes to serve it, turn the soufflé out on a serving dish, pour the sauce over it. Mrs. Appleyard likes a few chopped blanched almonds sprinkled over it but this is not necessary.

Foamy Sauce

½ cup butter
1 cup powdered sugar
yolks of 3 eggs and 1 whole egg

2 tablespoons sherry or brandy
or 1 teaspoon vanilla or ½
teaspoon almond

This has to be made at the last minute, but the butter, softened slightly, the sugar and flavoring may be combined beforehand and put in the top of a double boiler. When the time comes to serve it, beat the egg yolks and egg well, add them to the butter and sugar mixture and cook over hot water, beating all the time, until the mixture thickens. It takes only a few minutes.

The great advantage of this sauce is that someone undoubtedly clears the table for you while you are making it. Mrs. Appleyard graciously accepts this service provided it is clearly understood that no plates are stacked before rinsing. A plate that has, for instance, Hollandaise on the bottom as well as the top has an unfortunate effect on this lady's disposition.

Everybody's disposition is pretty good when the sauce is ready.

Vermont Cheese Soup
(FOR A COOL EVENING)

Mrs. Appleyard likes to make this soup with cheese from the neighboring town of Cabot, but she admits that it can be made using real dairy cheese from New York or Wisconsin. She would rather not discuss the topic of processed cheese since the subject has an unfortunate influence on her blood pressure. She simply states, more in anger than in sorrow, that she hopes everyone who likes it has a piece of aerated plaster of Paris bread to eat with it.

She begins her soup by cutting finely:

½ cup celery   ½ cup onion
½ cup carrots from the garden   ½ cup green pepper

These she cooks gently in ¼ cup butter or chicken fat till the onion is tender and pale gold in color. Then add 2 cups chicken stock and let it simmer.

While the vegetables are cooking she makes this sauce:

6 tablespoons butter   1 quart rich Vermont milk or
6 tablespoons flour   3 cups ordinary milk and 1
salt and pepper to taste   cup cream
                1 cup grated cheese

Melt the butter. Blend in the flour. Reduce heat; blend in the milk and cream. Add cheese and seasonings — salt, pepper, a pinch of mixed herbs. (Mrs. Appleyard doesn't add anything.) The vegetables should not be mushy but slightly crisp so by the time the sauce is ready you may put the two mixtures together into your best Dutch or Swedish enameled iron dish to heat. Stir and serve. *But* in corn season add just before serving a cup of Golden Bantam Corn cut from ears cooked 10 minutes.

Brown bread sandwiches are good with this or a long loaf of French bread cut part way through, spread with garlic butter and heated, or Graham Sour Milk Bread.

Graham Sour Milk Bread

Every now and then Mrs. Appleyard has a yearning for the kind of Graham bread her grandmother used to make. The secret was never written down. Apparently in those times everyone knew how to make it, just as before 1840 everyone knew how to design and build an attractive, comfortable durable house. The houses and the bread were both so simple that it seems to have been assumed that there was no mystery about either worth investigating or recording. Mrs. Appleyard has done little about the houses, merely gritting her teeth and groaning loudly when she sees another innocent structure being covered with imitation brick siding, but she keeps chasing a dream called Grandmother's Graham Bread.

She doesn't expect it to come true and she offers this formula as merely a reasonable facsimile and to make it easier for her own descendants to recapture their grandmother's cooking.

5½ cups Graham flour
¾ cup sugar
3 teaspoons soda
1½ cups molasses
3 cups white flour

1½ teaspoons salt
3 teaspoons baking powder
3 cups sour milk (part cream if possible)

Mix and sift dry ingredients. Stir in first the molasses, then the sour milk. Beat well. Put into greased pans, filling them two thirds full and bake for one hour. Start at 375° and when the loaves are well risen, reduce the heat to 350°.

Glazed Carrots

Carrots pulled out of the garden and cooked within half an hour are a very different item from the blasé vegetable, homesick for California or Texas, sulking in a ventilated plastic bag, that is commonly found in our larders. They are good cut into matchstick pieces and eaten raw, good grated raw with onions and cabbage as salad, good sliced paper thin and sautéed in butter and then simmered in water, especially good, Mrs. Appleyard thinks, glazed. She allows two small carrots for each person.

12 small carrots   1 onion, minced
1 cup hot water   3 tablespoons butter
3 tablespoons light brown sugar   ¼ teaspoon nutmeg
1 teaspoon lemon juice   2 tablespoons chopped mint
                        salt to taste

Scrub the carrots, slice them. Sauté them and the onion in
the butter. Add the water and sugar, cover, simmer 10 minutes.
Uncover and cook 10 to 15 minutes longer. Add the lemon
juice, nutmeg, salt if you like it. By this time they should be
nicely glazed. Add the mint (or substitute parsley or chopped
chives) and serve. Maple syrup or honey may be substituted
for the brown sugar. Serves six.

Appointment with Orion

Moon-viewing, Cicely reported to her mother and sister
one temperate August evening, is much esteemed among the
Japanese. Congenial groups of people meet at certain well-
favored spots to watch the moon rise. They take along special
foods such as hot rice wine, bean curd, pickled radishes . . .

"A most aesthetic sort of picnic," said Mrs. Appleyard, who
was stretched out on her red and white quilt, entertaining her

daughters at an informal soirée. "Shall we greet the harvest moon with pumpkin pie and new cider?"

"I wasn't thinking so much of saluting the moon in this fashion. Have you had your appointment with Orion yet?"

Cicely referred to Mrs. Appleyard's well-known fondness for getting up in the black crispness of late August nights in order to see Orion haul himself over the eastern horizon for the first time since he vanished in the west the previous spring.

"Well, no," said her mother. "I've been sleeping particularly well lately. But it is just about time for him to appear."

"I challenge you to Orion-viewing, then," said Cicely. "The loser has to bring suitable refreshments to the winner's house."

"No matter what the hour?" Mrs. Appleyard gave a slight moan.

"No matter what the hour," said Cicely firmly. "The one who sees Orion first will telephone to the other, and the loser will then turn up as soon as possible with the appropriate picnic materials."

"I'm leaving at the end of the week," said Sally hastily. She had come over from Roland Hill for a brief holiday from the music school. "Please don't include me in your riotous goings-on. I am sure the night air would not agree with what ails me. I might even sneeze." As Sally often sneezed thirty or forty times when she got started, this was no mean threat.

"We wouldn't dream of exposing you to a sneeze. Anyway, no one should come who doesn't want to. It would spoil the single-minded rapture of the viewers." Cicely uncoiled herself from the small red chair and prepared to depart. She is not one of those who say "I must go" and then hover for half an hour on the doorstep.

"You don't suppose the ringing of the telephone about 3 A.M.

will dislocate the neighborhood?" asked Mrs. Appleyard. "Otherwise I accept your challenge. Cheesecake, perhaps, at thirty paces?"

"Aline Pocock is the only one who will lift her receiver. She told me once she never had time to listen in during the day, but at night she just couldn't resist those long-distance rings. It will certainly give her something to ponder if she hears that Orion has come to town."

Cicely was at the door now. "Just the right sort of night," she added. "I had better get right home. I don't want to be caught without suitable star-viewing materials."

It was not that night, however, but one several evenings later that the telephone by Cicely's bed began its insistent five-beat ring. She struggled up out of sleep to hear her mother's quietly triumphal tones announcing: "The password is Orion."

No one on the party line could possibly have had time to hear this one-sided conversation, Cicely thought, as she struggled into a skirt and sweater, slipped on her sandals and went to the kitchen to pick up the picnic basket which had stood ready for star-viewing since the evening the challenge had been issued. It was the same tea basket that had accompanied the Bradshaws and the Appleyards on their tour around England in the late 30's. They would not need the spirit lamp, but Cicely filled the Thermos with a spiced fruit punch made with a mild tea base, to be served hot. In the sandwich box she put star-shaped cookies of rich, buttery shortbread and larger star-shaped sandwiches of her own version of Anadama bread filled with cream cheese, chives from her kitchen doorstep and a little grated carrot. There were a couple of pieces of preserved ginger in a twist of silver foil to complete the menu.

By the time Cicely had driven from Birch Hill to her mother's house at Appleyard Center Mrs. Appleyard was out on the porch in her ancient camel's-hair dressing gown. The light was on in the summer kitchen and a small fire was whispering in the Glenwood heater.

"You were quick," said Mrs. Appleyard as she greeted her daughter. "I didn't expect you for five minutes at least. See, our friend has pulled himself head and shoulders above the sugarplace." The slow beat of late cicadas blended with the steady roar of water over Mrs. Appleyard's dam in the pasture brook. Cicely went in to heat the spiced tea and came out again with one of her mother's bird-of-paradise painted trays set with Wedgwood.

"I wish I had a *sake* bottle and little white cups," she said. "You will have to imagine that this is rice wine. I didn't have time to pickle any radishes either."

They sat on the porch for nearly an hour, sipping, talking, nibbling and watching, till the stars began to fade in the first gray light of dawn, and the birds began to stir in the syringa bushes. With the first light wind of the day Cicely began to sneeze.

"I hope I am not allergic to Orion," she managed to say as she rummaged for a Kleenex. "Sally was most prophetic."

"Leave everything and go right home," said her mother hospitably. "I'll see you next year."

MENUS FOR STAR-VIEWING

Cicely's
Hot Spiced Fruit Punch * (D.M.)
Shortbread

Cream Cheese and Chives Sandwiches on Anadama Bread *
Preserved Ginger

Mrs. Appleyard's
Hot Sanka in a Thermos
Thin Scalded Johnny Cake *
Watercress Sandwiches *
Madeleines, Soft Chocolate Frosting *

Hot Spiced Fruit Punch (D.M.)

Boil 5 minutes:	1 teaspoon allspice
2 cups sugar	Add 4 rounded teaspoons tea
2 cups water	12 whole cloves
	2-inch stick of cinnamon

Cover. Let stand ten minutes. Strain. Add: 1½ cups orange
juice, ¾ cup lemon juice, 4 quarts water. Heat and serve.
Serves twelve.

Cicely's Anadama Bread

½ cup yellow corn meal	½ cup molasses
2 cups boiling water	1 yeast cake
1 teaspoon salt	½ cup lukewarm water
3 tablespoons lard or bacon fat	1 teaspoon sugar
	5 cups sifted flour

Sprinkle the cornmeal slowly into the rapidly boiling water;
cook 5 minutes, stirring all the time. Add salt, shortening, molasses; cool to lukewarm. Dissolve yeast and sugar in lukewarm

water. Add 2 cups of the flour and beat well. Add the rest of the flour or enough to make a stiff dough. Knead well; let it rise till double in size. Shape two loaves, let rise again and bake at 375°. This bread has an unusual flavor and is good eaten plain or with some sort of cheese.

Thin Scalded Johnny Cake

1 cup corn meal, yellow or white	extra butter, about 2 tablespoons
1 cup boiling water — more if needed	salt to taste
2 tablespoons butter	Crisco for greasing pans

Light the oven — 475°. Put the corn meal, butter and the salt into a bowl. Bring it close to your rapidly boiling water. It should be as hot as possible when it strikes the meal. Pour the water over the meal a little at a time, returning the saucepan of water to the fire after each addition. When the butter has melted and the meal has absorbed all the water it will take, put small lumps of the batter on a greased baking sheet and spread them out as thin as you can. Use a broad round-ended knife or a spatula for this and dip it into hot water from time to time. Put a dot of butter in the middle of each cake. Bake until they are brown — about 10 minutes. It is perhaps unnecessary to say that when Mrs. Appleyard looks at them at the end of 5 minutes and finds that they do not look buttery enough, she adds some more. Remove the cakes from the sheet with a spatula as soon as they are done. Immediately. You may break some but such manavelins make agreeable eating. They are best when served hot but they are good cold too and will keep crisp for some time in a closed tin box. They can always be reheated briefly but there are not usually enough left to have this problem arise.

Mrs. Appleyard does not plan to stop and reheat them when she goes constellation-viewing at dawn next year.

Watercress Sandwiches

It must be a great surprise to watercress, Mrs. Appleyard thinks, to find itself one minute growing where Venetia Hopkins' spring runs into her brook and ten minutes later being suddenly made into sandwiches and seasoned with garlic and horseradish. Then, because there was some left, being sharp-frozen in her deep freeze, remaining inert until she prudently thawed them out one evening she thought Orion might be planning an early morning visit. What a peaceful pastoral life this innocent vegetation lived until Mrs. Appleyard found out it was there.

Unluckily for the watercress, there had been a food sale and there was a lot of homemade bread on hand that responded pleasantly to being sliced thin. There was Green Mayonnaise (p. 73) which had been made in the electric blender with 2 cloves of garlic and a dash of horseradish added to it. Also there was sweet butter soft enough to spread. Mrs. Appleyard cuts the cress up with scissors and mixes it with the mayonnaise.

She says you can make the sandwiches very satisfactorily even out of watercress that did not grow among mint and forget-me-nots at the edge of a brook that runs past seven elms with orioles in them. Sadly we admit that this is probably true.

Madeleines

4 eggs
1 cup sugar, sifted
1 cup cake flour
powdered sugar, or whatever
    frosting you like

½ cup butter, melted
1 teaspoon vanilla
1 teaspoon baking powder

Mrs. Appleyard had forgotten all about madeleines until she saw an unusual cake pan among Venetia Hopkins' baking tins.

"What is this wonderful heavy pan that seems to have sea shells pressed into it?" she asked. Venetia said it was a madeleine pan, from France.

"You know — the cake Proust dipped in his tea," she added.

"May I make some?" Mrs. Appleyard asked. "Then we can dunk them in our tea and perhaps pretty soon we'll remember enough fascinating circumstances so we'll each write a seven-volume classic."

Venetia supplied suitable encouragement to this project and Mrs. Appleyard got a copy of her own cookbook off the shelf —it was standing, she noticed proudly, right next to Escoffier — and went to work.

"It says here that they are easy to make," she reported confidently, for she had a childlike trust in printed words, even her own, especially after she had corrected and improved them. She did just what the book said. She dusted the pans lightly with flour. She lit the oven — 400°. She melted the butter but did not let it boil. She sifted the flour, measured it, then sifted it with the baking powder three times more. She sifted the sugar, beat the eggs well, and beat the sugar into them. Then she added the melted butter and beat it into the batter with the vanilla. Last of all she stirred in the flour. She filled the pans half full of batter, set them in the oven and baked the cakes until they sprang back when touched in the middle, about 15 minutes. There were two dozen.

She frosted some and sprinkled the others with powdered sugar. These were the ones she and Venetia dipped in their tea that afternoon. Perhaps fortunately, no literary trances in seven volumes have followed this experience.

Can there be something wrong with the rule?

Venetia says they tasted all right but perhaps some secret ingredient was lacking. If anyone can supply its name Mrs. Appleyard will be most grateful and promises not to publish it in her revised edition, but just to write it in the margin of her own copy. She uses a rather faint tired pencil. How does she always happen to have one — and an unco-operative pen — on hand? Well, that's her secret.

Soft Chocolate Frosting

1 teaspoon instant coffee, dissolved in 1 teaspoon hot water
1 square Baker's Chocolate
1 egg, beaten
1 tablespoon butter, creamed

1 teaspoon vanilla
1½ tablespoons thick Vermont cream
2 cups confectioners' sugar, sifted

Add the chocolate to the coffee and cook over hot water until the chocolate is melted. Beat the egg and stir the melted chocolate into it. Add the softened butter and beat in the sugar gradually. Beat in the cream and the vanilla. Spread on the cakes — they should be cool. Decorate with pecan halves or scatter chopped walnut meats over them.

September

Goodbye to a House

ONE OF THE most unusual occasions that Cicely and Mrs.
Appleyard have ever attended was a farewell party for a house.
It occurred early in September, at the season when those who
have spent the summer in rented houses are suddenly persuaded
that their lives will be incomplete unless they own a century-old
Cape-Cod-Vermont-style farmhouse with superb view and in-
adequate water, like all the rest of the summer colony. (Winter
residents have traded view for water in a spirit of necessitous
compromise, though some more fortunate, like Cicely and
Geoffrey Toussaint, are blessed with both.)

Barbara and Frank Larned were most notably infected that summer with the need to link their fates with that of Appleyard Center. They were handy with maps and found their way along the web of back roads with enviable skill. Cicely suggested for them Louis Lombard's faded yellow house and foaming trout brook, but somehow, Bar said regretfully, it did not speak to them. The murmur of the brook could not overcome the small sad voice of a house in shadows, sturdy and straight though it was. Perhaps too many people had been lonely there.

It had not been necessary, therefore, to explain to the Larneds that on Saturday nights this particular house was the unwilling target of high-spirited drivers trying to get home from Saffords' Barn Dance, and that quite often one or more cars did not make the curve by the bridge and landed in Louis' dooryard, requiring chains, shovels and occasionally bandages and sheriffs.

The relations of houses with people are as complex as those of human beings with other human beings. The Larneds found for themselves a house which spoke a language they understood and it was love at first sight. But, alas, someone else had found the beloved beautiful, a Frenchwoman (from Paris, France, said Roger, as usual the fount of information and misinformation, distinguished in this way, no doubt, from Paris, Maine), who was going to raise cats, chickens and canaries and live there all the year round. She was variously described as a widow-woman and as a wife whose husband traveled a good deal. Time would tell.

The house was the old Bass place, part of the Bass family for more than a hundred years. It hurt Cranston and Lily to the quick to have to sell it, but sell it they must, for it had stood empty for three years and they could only come for an occasional weekend. Cranston could farm no longer and they had to live in a village near work for Lily — she was a fine teacher. As for Cranston's sister, Sara — it was understood that she did not care for the idea at all, and probably would not come again unless they kept the grove of birches that startled the eye each time it came into view.

Sara had always reminded Cicely and Mrs. Appleyard of Emily Dickinson. She was not only a poet, she was poetry itself, a flame in a tiny lamp. Ferns were her friends; she talked the language of birds readily, more shyly and hesitantly that of human beings, so that she took refuge in music and in reading when she was not out walking through the birches, or testing one of the Bass farm sunsets against some inner standard.

The Bass house and its setting spoke loud and clear to the Larneds. There was even the perfect place for a studio-work-shop for Frank in the shape of a little old schoolhouse just across the road. They kept going back to the isolated hilltop and its widespread mountain prospect with a wistfulness which appealed greatly to the Bass family, who said frankly that they would have much preferred it if the Larneds could have had the house. Oh, they liked Marissa Peckham well enough, but she was different somehow; the Larneds were much more their kind of folks. Still, Mrs. Peckham had claimed the house first.

Cicely, as real estate agent, a role she occasionally adopted for the fun of it, though she generally described herself as more of an anti-real estate agent, was somewhat involved in the proceedings. Thus it came about that she and Mrs. Appleyard were climbing a steep stretch of abandoned road one sunny quiet afternoon early in September, their goal the last appearance of the Bass farm as such.

The Larneds had already arrived when Cicely and her mother came up the last almost perpendicular slope. So had Mrs. Peckham, a bright-eyed dark-haired woman who looked far too slender to survive a Vermont winter all alone in a big house four miles from the village and with no close neighbors. As the Larneds had been to Paris, France, they were able to converse with their triumphant rival about their affection for her native city.

In a minute or two the Basses appeared with materials for a tea which could certainly be called High. For the last time Cranston brought in wood from the shed and Lily made a fire in the polished black stove. The old kettle hissed and hummed. Cicely noticed that like the Appleyards they kept marbles in it to keep the hard water from encrusting it too deeply. You could hear them roll when Lily lifted it to fill the painted earthenware teapot that Mrs. Appleyard had admired for some years.

On the round walnut table was spread a fringed damask cloth; pink luster cups were set out with thin silver spoons beside them. There were plates of chicken sandwiches made with fine-grained white bread. There was a special apricot preserve with a mysterious flavor. Finger lengths of fruit cake, moist with fruit, starred with nuts, lay on a Sandwich glass plate. A many-layered, maple-frosted cake stood beside it. Hot toasted and buttered Montpelier crackers came in relays from the wood stove to serve as base for the apricot preserve.

After the teapot had been filled and emptied several times and the guests could hold no more, Mrs. Bass asked each one to choose something from the house as a remembrance. Mrs. Appleyard, too ladylike to ask for the painted teapot, chose a pair of carved walnut brackets. Cicely asked for the round blue-spotted covered butter dish. The Larneds cherished a plaster of Paris cat with an Egyptian smile. To Mrs. Peckham the Basses left all kinds of furniture, including a large number of beds.

"Perhaps she is going to have other guests than those in feathers and fur," suggested Cicely as she and Mrs. Appleyard and the Larneds strolled along the firm grass-centered road for a last look at the ghostly stems of the birches.

"I prophesy that she won't last out the first winter," said Mrs. Appleyard. "The cats will eat the canaries, she will eat the chickens, and solitude will eat her."

Time would tell.

MENU FOR A FAREWELL TEA

Chicken Sandwiches on Homemade Bread *
Montpelier Crackers Toasted and Buttered
Apricot Preserve
Fruit Cake
Maple Layer Cake *
Tea

Bread (W.H.)

A generation brought up more and more on bread made of plaster of Paris, old absorbent cotton and almost edible sponges has duly revolted and makes its own bread. Cicely notes that almost as many men of her acquaintance are skilled breadmakers as women. She has extracted the secret of his success from the best baker (amateur) that she knows. Herewith his directions. He says:

I make this with an electric mixer, but I've done it on occasion without; doesn't seem to make much difference.

For two pound and a half loaves:

Dissolve one or two envelopes of dry yeast (two to make it faster) in two cups of lukewarm water.

Add enough dry-milk powder (varies according to the brand) to make a pint of milk. Mix it until it dissolves. Add two tablespoons of margarine or butter. Add an egg. Then two tablespoons of sugar, one tablespoon of salt and four tablespoons of honey. If you've kept the mixer going, you can then start adding flour, otherwise get this all mixed first.

Use from six to seven and a half cups of King Arthur unbleached all-purpose flour. With the mixer you can put in about three cups of it before the batter starts to climb the beaters; then I take out one beater and continue to mix at low speed plus a rubber scraper. The last cup or so of flour you have to knead by hand.

The dough tends to be sticky (honey and egg) but don't make the mistake of adding too much flour in an attempt to overcome this, or you'll get too dry a loaf. Kneading — ten to fifteen minutes — will get rid of some but not all of the stickiness.

Let the bread rise in a bowl greased with Crisco or something similar, over a pan with hot water in it, out of drafts. (The cover can be a dish towel.) It will double in size in anywhere from an hour to three or so, depending on such things as warmth, humidity, the collusion of the planets, and your own impatience. When it is about twice its original size, punch it down, fold the edges to the middle, and turn the lump over. Let it rise again. It's a lot quicker the second time — usually.

Then make loaves. There are lots of ways. A simple one is to divide the dough into four parts, knead each one into a ball, and put two such balls into each greased loaf pan. More complicated (but some people say it makes a smoother loaf) is to flatten it out, fold it in thirds, flatten that out, fold it in thirds and so on. When I get the loaves made, I puncture them all over the top with a fork, which is supposed to let out air bubbles (maybe it does) and makes a nice pattern. Then the loaves have to rise till they're double in size (an hour or so), again covered and in a warm place.

I preheat the oven to 375°, put in the bread and set the timer for ten minutes. When it buzzes, I cut the thermostat down to 325° and set the timer for half an hour. Look at the bread sometime around the twenty to thirty minute mark and if it seems to be too brown, turn the thermostat to 300°.

Take the bread out, and out of the pans. Cool it on a wire rack. While it's still hot (just as soon as you get it on the rack) brush the tops of the loaves with Mazola or melted butter.

That's the story. One note: probably because of the honey, this bread keeps very well, especially if it's airtight-wrapped in wax paper and kept in the refrigerator.

Cicely can vouch that this makes a fine-grained sweet-tasting loaf, that cuts well, toasts well and tastes — well, like bread.

Apricots

Mrs. Appleyard has not yet focused her crystal ball so that she has been able to report just what is it that makes the Bass apricot preserve so particularly excellent — Cicely suspects lemon peel and a little almond extract are involved — but she has some suggestions about how to use apricots. It became necessary for her to be ingenious about apricots because she had fallen absent-mindedly into the habit of saying to herself in the super-market: "I ought to have some apricots in the house," and putting a package into her wire basket. When she was confronted one day with five packages on her cupboard shelf, the idea dawned on her gradually that she had better use some of them. These were some of the ways:

Apricot Sauce

An electric blender is a great help in making apricots into pulp. Use dried apricots, the tenderized kind (Mrs. Appleyard hates the word and all its sisters, cousins, aunts and brothers-in-law!). Follow the directions on the package but do not drain off the water. The blender works better with water. When the apricots are tender, put them into the blender. Do not put too many in at a time but do them in rather small batches, using part of the liquid each time and running the blender about 2 minutes. You now have a fine bowl of pulp to use as you like.

For Apricot Sauce, take:

1 cup apricot pulp	juice and grated rind of half a
½ cup sugar	lemon

Stir the sugar with the warm apricot pulp until it is thoroughly dissolved. Add the lemon juice and the rind. Taste it and add more sugar if you like it very sweet. Serve it as sauce for orange sherbet or vanilla ice cream.

Apricot Soufflé

3 tablespoons butter
1 cup milk, scalded
⅓ cup sugar
a little vanilla or almond ex-
    tract, or both, or neither

1 tablespoon butter extra
¼ cup flour
½ cup apricot pulp
5 eggs, separated

Melt the butter, turn off the heat and rub in the flour. Light the oven: 350°. Put the extra tablespoon of butter in a heat-proof glass dish and set it into a pan of warm water in the oven. Stir the scalded milk into the butter and flour mixture. Do it slowly, stirring all the time so there are no lumps. (If there are, you must strain them out.) Cool the mixture slightly. Add the apricot pulp mixed with the sugar and flavoring. Beat the egg yolks thick and lemon-colored and mix in thoroughly. Beat the egg whites stiff and dry. Fold gently into the mixture. Mrs. Appleyard does it with what Venetia Hopkins calls the Spendthrift's Enemy — a rubber scraper. She uses it also to heap the mixture lightly in the warmed dish.

Put the dish back in the pan of water. You should put a rack or the top of a Crisco can under the soufflé. Bake it at 350° for 20 minutes on the lowest shelf of the oven. Then reduce the heat to 325° and transfer the dish to the upper shelf. You may breathe while you do this, but not hard. The soufflé is done when it no longer hisses when you listen to it. This will take another 25 minutes. Perhaps a little more. As in the case of every other soufflé, the customers must wait for it, not the other way. They usually seem perfectly willing, Mrs. Appleyard says.

Apricot Soufflé in the Double Boiler

For a change Mrs. Appleyard sometimes makes the less nerve-racking kind of soufflé like the orange kind (p. 148). She uses apricot pulp sweetened and flavored with almond instead of the orange marmalade.

Apricot Rolls

At the time there was a large bowl of apricot pulp in Mrs. Appleyard's refrigerator she received from one of her favorite philosophers a package containing sugary apricot-flavored rolls apparently constructed of thin sheets of apricot. They came from Charleston, S.C., where the philosopher, who just to make things confusing is delightfully feminine in the French marquise style and is called Sheldon Beauregard, says they are called Peach Leather. By the time Mrs. Appleyard got this information and an invitation to join the Pythagorean Society, she had already made a pretty good facsimile. This is how.

    1 package (11 ounces) dried quick-cooking apricots
    1 cup sugar
    extra sugar for rolling — about a cup

Cover the apricots with water and cook them until they are quite soft, 15 to 20 minutes. Either drain most of the water off and put them through the meat grinder, using the finest cutter, or make them into pulp in the electric blender (p. 170). What you want is a fine, smooth apricot pulp, not too wet, not too dry. Light the oven — 450°. Add the cup of sugar to the apricot pulp. Put the mixture into an aluminum saucepan and stir it over a low flame until the sugar is melted. Now spread it as thin as possible on ungreased cooky sheets or in very shallow cooky pans. Half the amount given will cover two 10 x 14 sheets. It should be spread so thin that you should see the metal through it as if you were looking through colored cellophane. When it is as thin as you can possibly get it, put the sheets into the oven. After 5 minutes reverse their positions in the oven, upper one on the lower shelf, lower one on the upper shelf, turn off the heat and leave them to dry overnight.

In the morning the pulp should be dry enough to roll. If it is not dry enough so that it can be lifted from the pan with a spatula and hold its shape, light the oven again for a few minutes, turn it off and leave the pans for another half hour. The pulp should feel just slightly tacky. It should be a little less sticky than Scotch tape and not much thicker.

Now score it neatly with your spatula into 2 x 3 inch pieces. Sprinkle it all over with sugar. Put some more sugar on a shallow plate. Spread wax paper over the table before you begin. This is a sit-down job. Mrs. Appleyard, never fond of doing one thing at a time if two are convenient, places herself in front of a window where she can see blue jays battling over the smörgåsbord she has prepared for their entertainment and hers.

With the spatula remove the apricot oblongs and lay them one at a time, unsugared side down, in the plate of sugar. Roll them as tightly as you can in the sugar. Have a candy box lined with wax paper ready. Pack the rolls in neatly, sprinkling sugar between the layers and separating the layers with wax paper.

If you like apricots, Mrs. Appleyard is pretty sure you will like these.

Prune Tortoiseshell

No sooner had Mrs. Appleyard conquered the apricot rolls than it occurred to her that prunes might be treated in the same way. So she took:

1 pound quick-cooking prunes	½ cup sugar
juice and thin peel of half a lemon	more sugar for rolling, about 1 cup

Simmer the prunes until it is easy to remove the pits — about half an hour. Then use exactly the same method as with the apricot roll-ups in the preceding recipe. You may roll them around blanched almonds or toasted almonds, Mrs. Appleyard says. She adds that she sees no reason why strawberry pulp shouldn't be treated the same way. After all, even if the strawberry season was over, there were still strawberries in the freezer. And wonderful peaches from Virginia in the market.

"You've done enough," Patience Barlow said gently but firmly.

She was washing the pans and it seems Mrs. Appleyard had left one of them in the oven too long. It was covered with a substance that could have been made into a tortoiseshell cigarette box without not much more trouble than it took to get it off the pan. It would have been easy to cut the whole thing up with a hacksaw, or anyway with an acetylene torch.

It was Patience who gave the confection its name.

Mrs. Appleyard sensibly decided to use the peaches in ice cream or pandowdy or shortcake. It was weeks before she rolled anything more complicated than a sugar cooky.

Strawberry Roll-Ups

However, Mrs. Appleyard could not forget her curiosity about strawberries. She did not sacrifice her own Appleyard Center strawberries but used:

1 12-ounce box of frozen straw-   sugar for rolling, about ¾ cup
berries

She thawed the strawberries, poured them into the electric blender and ran it until they were thoroughly puréed. The resulting pulp was rather moister than the apricot or the prune pulp so she poured it into a shallow aluminum pan. It would have run off a cooky sheet. She distributed it evenly simply by tipping the pan from side to side, put the pan into the oven at 450° and turned it off after 5 minutes. In the morning the pulp was still too sticky to handle so she lighted the oven again at 250° and turned it off after 5 minutes. In about half an hour the pulp was tacky enough but not too sticky. She marked it into 2 x 3 inch oblongs and got them off the pans.

During this period she was heard to murmur a few rhetorical questions such as: "Why did I get mixed up in such an affair again?"

However, she felt much better pleased with the world when she had sugared, rolled and packed them and had tried one that was slightly frayed around the edges. She served them for dessert the next day with cream cheese, broken up with a fork and with thick Vermont cream stirred into it. About that time, Cicely reports, Mrs. Appleyard was heard telling her friends that it really was no trouble at all.

Ho! Hum!

Stirabout Maple Cake (L.P.)

1 egg	1 cup soft maple sugar
1 cup sour cream	½ teaspoon soda
2 cups flour	1 teaspoon cinnamon
¼ teaspoon nutmeg	½ teaspoon salt

Light the oven — 375°. Sift the flour four times with the dry ingredients. Beat the egg. Beat in the maple sugar. Stir in the sour cream and the flour mixture. Bake in two greased layer cake pans until the cake shrinks from the edges and springs back when pressed with the finger — about 20 minutes.

Frosting

Into a measuring cup stir together ⅓ cup sugar and ⅔ cup maple syrup. Cook this slowly to soft-ball stage. Use a candy thermometer and don't turn your back or it will be all over the stove. Mrs. Appleyard christened her new gas range in this sweet and expensive way. "What gas range is this?" asked Cicely as she unthinkingly typed these words. "Did you win it in a contest?" "Oh," said her mother airily. "I'm thinking of entering the Sillsbury Baking Contest. The least you can get is a new stove. Or perhaps Our Book will be so successful ..." "This is the first I've heard of writing up stoves before they are installed," said Cicely. But she let the sentence stand. She is a dutiful daughter, and besides there was a strong likelihood that by the time the book was printed, a splendid gas range would indeed grace the Summer Kitchen. Cicely had watched her mother operate for some years and knew that her lightest word could bring about astonishing results though not always just those she had planned on.

Back to the frosting, which is about to boil over. Beat 2 egg whites well. Pour on the cooked syrup gradually and keep beating until the frosting is cool. If the frosting strikes you as too sweet add a pinch of salt to your beaten egg whites. Use this on top of the cake and between the layers. Decorate with pecan halves, or with butternuts.

Labor Day Dance

THE LABOR DAY WEEKEND is a complicated one in Appleyard Center, what with the theatrical producers dashing up from Broadway for a last breath of fresh air before sealing themselves hermetically in theaters and smoke-filled rooms, the Music School geniuses getting ready for Carnegie Hall and children needing new shoes and haircuts before school starts. No motion picture camera can do justice to its various activities.

Mrs. Appleyard gives some of the haircuts and pays the customers according to the quantity of hair involved and how still they sit. Tommy Bradshaw received fifty cents for almost enough hair to stuff a small pillow. Extravagantly Mrs. Appleyard swept it off the porch and into the asters, where, she states, chipping sparrows will find it next year if they need it.

Hair is an interesting substance, she says. It varies not only in color but in diameter, texture, curliness and how it grows. She has had ample opportunity to observe these variations since she cut both her sons' hair until they went to college, and that of any friends they brought home. She did not pay that generation so she feels it is only fair that she should occasionally make use of the information thus acquired in one of the mystery stories she writes.

She has been working lately on an item called "Death of a Dancer." Inspired perhaps by this title, she decided to add to the Labor Day complications by giving a dance. She chose the ballroom of the old tavern at Roland Hill for this festivity, and enlisted her daughters' co-operation. Mrs. Appleyard has a peculiarity. She likes to give parties but hates to give invitations. Her bargain with her daughters stipulated that she would engage the musicians, put new candles in the sconces, supply punch, oatmeal cookies and similar innocent refreshments, while they would invite about forty people. This arrangement was perfectly harmonious and resulted in sixty-six guests answering to the scrape of Robin Viereck's fiddle.

He, of course, was the most important guest, and Mrs. Appleyard went in person to invite him. Music is only a sideline with Robin. His real interest is goats. Mrs. Appleyard was welcomed by a delegation of Nubians of distinguished lineage. For all she knows they may be descendants of the original goats that people had to tell the sheep from. Robin gets sixteen quarts of milk from them, he told her.

"Where do you sell it?" Mrs. Appleyard asked.

"Well, I don't have much luck selling it," Robin said. "I drink what I can and the rest I run through again. It gets real strengthening after a while. If I'd only begun drinking goats' milk about seventy-eight years ago I'd have been pretty rugged by now. Probably."

Evidently the goats throve on their own milk. That is, if activity means anything. When Mrs. Appleyard came out there were five Nubians on her new car: one on the hood, one on the luggage compartment, and two on the roof. With the towering white cloud-mountains in the sky, the cold blue mountains below, the rocky hillside, the green lake and Robin's brown cottage tucked under the hill, the effect was charmingly Swiss.

"Lucky I keep them manicured," observed their owner. "Just start the motor — they'll jump."

Mrs. Appleyard was relieved to learn that her car would not be scarred or permanently decorated in the style of a Swiss alp. She started the motor. There was a noise of dancing hooves. Lithe sleek brown forms filled the air around her. A buck reared up at the window and tried to get in the front seat with her.

"He likes you," Robin said.

Indifferent to this compliment, Mrs. Appleyard raised the window hastily and drove off.

She stopped at the store for her mail. As she came out she was affectionately greeted by the Nubians. They had strolled down for their mail too, she supposed. They stepped on her feet and seemed delighted to see her. So did a large hissing gander and his long-necked family.

"Goats and ganders adored her," murmured Mrs. Appleyard, making her way through this crowd of admirers. She was carrying three gallons of ice cream — vanilla, butter pecan and banana almond. Or perhaps they just like ice cream, she thought honestly. I wonder if they'll come to the party.

Mrs. Appleyard's pastoral popularity was ephemeral. Not a

Nubian appeared in the ballroom of the Tavern. The first footsteps were those of her grandchildren, who came early to polish the floor. They scattered something called Spangles out of a box and slid over it screaming happily until the place was like a skating rink. The room was lighted by a pink glow from the west and a yellow moon from the east. It is a long room with small-paned windows along three walls and a fireplace at each end. Old chairs and benches in soft yellow line the gray and green walls, on which hang old portraits and prints and tin candle sconces.

Mrs. Appleyard had put new candles in the sconces, an exercise during which she usually calls down a short blessing upon the memory of Thomas Alva Edison. Candlelight is picturesque, and, if you are over twenty-three, merciful. Still, after you have dealt with forty-two candleholders of different types, it is restful to know that there is an invention by which you can turn a switch and have a light come on that neither smokes nor drips wax upon the Steinway.

The dance followed the standard pattern for such festivities. At first it was a problem to get anyone on the floor. Later the question was how to find enough space on it for all the dancers. Distinguished guests with high I.Q.s and several degrees stumbled and confused their left hands with their right, while small children executed complex maneuvers with skill and style. Mrs. Appleyard was much pleased to be led out upon the sea of glass by a young gentlemen about three fourths her height, half her weight and one sixth her age.

"Did you have a good dance with Robert?" Tommy Bradshaw asked her.

"Yes, indeed, he dances very well," his grandmother said.

"I thought you'd like it. I told him to ask you," Tommy said.

Mrs. Appleyard has heard of brothers getting partners for their sisters, but this is the first example she knows of a grandson saving his grandmother from a wallflower's fate. She now turned her attention to the refreshments. One of the problems is to be sure that hollow-legged boys do not eat up everything before the less enterprising grownups appear. Mrs. Appleyard has a partial solution for this difficulty. She supplies at least five kinds of ice cream from the freezer and encourages the younger set to make their own cones in any wild combination of flavors that fancy dictates.

This is simply a delaying action. It does not mean that the younger guests will be indifferent to oatmeal lace cookies and fudge cake. It is just hurling the wolves something from the sleigh to distract them for a while.

"Ah," said Anstiss Baxter as she was offered a plate of meringues, "this is one of the items where to get one you have to show your birth certificate to prove you are over twenty-one."

This seemed like an excellent idea to Mrs. Appleyard. She plans to put it into practice another evening.

MENU FOR LIGHT REFRESHMENTS
DURING INTERMISSION

Ice Cream Bar *
Labor Day Punch (p. 54)
Oatmeal Cookies ‡
Walnut Cake *
Angel Cake (p. 33)
Brownies ‡
Fruit Cake ‡

Ice-Cream Bar

If she really had a bar it might be better, Mrs. Appleyard thinks, but as it would have to be twenty feet long to accommodate the ice-cream eaters perhaps it is better to keep on with the somewhat battered oval table in the Winter Kitchen. On this she puts four kinds of ice cream — vanilla, chocolate, maple walnut and black raspberry, for instance — the kinds they tell her at the Co-op are the popular favorites of the moment. She also puts out bowls of crushed strawberries or raspberries, chocolate sauce, maple syrup, chopped nuts. The possible combinations are difficult to estimate mathematically and of a kind calculated to make anyone over fifteen years old turn pale. The ice-cream fanciers, however, are not even slightly jaded by this simple type of hors d'oeuvre but are soon ready to get to work on any oatmeal cookies overlooked by their seniors and then dance quadrilles with renewed vigor.

Walnut Cake (L.P.) *(No Flour)*

1 pound walnuts weighed in the shell	6 eggs, separated
	1 cup powdered sugar
1 teaspoon baking powder	

Shell the walnuts and grind the meats. Add the baking powder. Light the oven — 375°. Beat the egg yolks, beat in the sugar, stir in the nuts. Whip the whites until they are stiff but not too dry and fold them into the mixture. Bake in two layers until the cakes shrink from the pans and spring back in the middle when touched. Cool and just before serving put whipped cream or mocha cream filling (p. 18) in between or on top. Or serve it cut in squares from a square pan, with whipped cream. Plan a light breakfast.

Ladies' Luncheon

THE INSTITUTION of the Ladies' Luncheon is one of the most pleasant in Appleyard Center and environs. This is partly because it takes place, as a rule, during the latter half of September, at a time when a mellow glow hangs over landscape and inhabitants alike: a mental glow arising from having cheated the frost of the last of the tomatoes and zinnias, completed another summer without disaster, said goodbye to the summer people fondly yet firmly; an interlude of relaxed peace before the first onset of winter.

Partly too because an assemblage of ladies has a flavor all its own and gives scope for a kind of social commentary not quite suited to mixed gatherings. So when Venetia Hopkins gave out invitations for a luncheon party in the third week of September, the Appleyard ladies knew they could look forward to elegant food in superior company.

Cicely was the last to arrive at the lunch party, driving up with a flourish and clatter in the 1931 Model A Ford that made her feel more like a fresh girl of twenty than the riper woman of forty that she really was. As she entered Venetia's comfortable kitchen she realized, however, that she could keep the illusion of youth for the afternoon, for none of the other ladies was under sixty, and some would not see eighty again.

All shades of gray hair were represented and all kinds of permanents, some more obviously homemade than others. Venetia and most of the rest had got out their tweeds for the occasion. In Vermont there are only about two weeks out of the year when it is comfortable to wear a tweed suit. This was the September tweed week; the other had come in early May. The Duncan sisters, however, had worn their gayest legislature silks.

"I don't know," said Daisy, settling her crocheted stole, "why I came out in this flimsy dress and a straw hat and dirty gloves." As always she looked as bright and neat as a small chickadee poised over sunflower seeds on a winter feeding tray. Fiona had her customary air of an efficient countess. Beatrice as usual reminded one of Einstein. Geoffrey Toussaint had a theory that all old ladies look like either Einstein or Thomas Jefferson, and Beatrice certainly bore him out.

"I often get real mean," she was murmuring. "Oh, you should just see how mean I am when I'm at home. Of course we all get that way sometimes. I wish I could go to Boston this winter and get a little room and just paint and paint and not have a soul tell me what to do." Cicely liked this picture of Beatrice imitating Gauguin in a Vermontish and feminine style. She wondered what the artistic bohemians of Boston would make of Beatrice's innocently fateful paintings.

The guests were helping themselves to Shrimp Jambalaya,

which bubbled in a huge frying pan on the shiny black stove, and to the hot rolls that had come from the Covered-Dish Supper at Appleyard Center, having spent a quiet two months in Venetia's freezer. They were Maria Flint's best and they tasted perhaps a little better even than when they were first baked. The freezer, brimming with summer souvenirs, had also yielded mushrooms picked in early August in Solon Marsh's back pasture. Watercress for the salad had been gathered by Venetia from her brook, and her special dressing was now soaking delicately the avocado slices, tomato quarters and mild onion rings that shared the enormous wooden salad bowl with late lettuce from her garden.

A happy luncheon silence had fallen over the company, and Cicely, who could always eat with greater expedition than anyone else, was the first to lift her head and take a long look at her fellow guests. This was strictly county society, she thought. Angela Thirkell should be here. As often happened she heard her mother begin to describe, across the room, how she had actually met Angela Thirkell during the past winter at a literary tea in Boston. This sort of extraverbal communication between Mrs. Appleyard and her eldest daughter might have become embarrassing over the years if they had had anything they wished desperately to conceal from each other.

Marietta Cushman from over the mountain seemed at first glance quite conventional. Yet she was actually one of the liveliest and most adventurous of the ladies, willing to patronize unpopular though worthy projects, which thus became acceptable in her village. She was a cousin of the Duncans, and both sides were pleased to acknowledge the relationship.

Cicely suspected that she herself was probably related to Marietta too. When she had first come to live in Appleyard

Center she had enjoyed discovering a new cousin each week and telling the children as they roamed around the countryside that such and such a house was inhabited by relations; but it was an old story by now, and it seemed more entertaining now to sit by, knowing you were connected with two thirds of the people in the room while neither side was in any particular hurry to claim the relationship.

"Are you very philosophical, Cicely?" a soft insistent voice asked at her elbow. It was fragile, earnest Cathie Winston, dim-sighted and poetic. What she might mean by her question bewildered Cicely for a moment, her thoughts having flown at once to Plato and Aristotle and beyond them to the pre-Socratics much mentioned by her sister Sally Roland on her last visit to Appleyard Center. Cicely held in considerable respect anyone on intimate terms with these philosophical heroes. However, it appeared that Cathie meant merely to inquire whether Cicely minded when her children screamed at her and called her names, and was reassured when Cicely told her she did not mind these assaults in the least and was able to give as good as she got.

It was time for dessert: Venetia's traditional plate of brownies, dark and melting, and a white cake dripping with icing and patterned with nuts, as well as pistachio ice cream and chocolate sauce.

"I'm thinking of selling my house," announced Lois Prince in ringing tones from across the room. "I'm tired of Mountain View, tired to death of it — I'm going far, far away."

"Oh, where?" asked Cicely with interest, for she was one of those who feels the departure of each train or bus a mortal wound if she is not aboard, and she was at once imagining Lois striding through a Turkish bazaar or banqueting on a Tahiti beach.

"Well," said Lois pensively. "I had thought of Great Barrington."

Cicely moved into the kitchen again, yielding her place on the comfortable yellow sofa to Mrs. Appleyard. A second cup of coffee was most welcome and she drank it sitting next to Rachel Benson who had exiled herself to the end of the kitchen table for spilling salad dressing down the front of her new blouse.

In spite of the misplaced condiments she looked fashionable and feminine as she remarked to Venetia: "Yes, I like to have something planned ahead. I've got twenty-five feet more of stone wall to lay, come spring. I've done fifty this summer. Any time I miss the Garden Club back in Ashtabula I go out and lay a couple of feet. I just *love* slate stone. The only trouble is that when Caspar Prout comes to fix the underpinning where it gets heaved by the frost he tries to borrow slate off my wall. That I will *not* have. He painted the ceiling of my porch blue, too, when I was home visiting mother in Ashtabula. I never could stand blue."

Cicely gazed at the pretty blue blouse which was now decorated with a trail of French dressing (plenty of garlic). She hoped Rachel would get a new blouse of a color she liked better and that she would stick to her guns, or rather her slates. They would make handy weapons if it came to a showdown.

The party was beginning to break up now. Mrs. Appleyard was collecting her mink scarf and arranging the heads and tails so that they lay in the proper directions. With her gray-blue suit she was wearing what is called in the local accounts of weddings matching accessories of cherry red — neat red calf shoes, a red sailor hat and a handsome red handbag that Cicely had given her last Christmas.

Cicely took great pride in her mother's chic appearance. It

had taken a good deal of frankly critical handwork on the part of Mrs. Appleyard's children to achieve this result. There was still a slight tendency for her slips to show, but perhaps in time this too would be corrected. Meanwhile they were extremely pretty slips. Cicely hoped that her own daughters would take an equal interest in seeing that she was well turned out. Till they reached the age of the cold eye and the tactful gibe she was quite happy in her unmatched stockings, slightly scuffed shoes and a five-year-old suit.

Jason Teasdale had already knocked discreetly at the kitchen door to let his wife know that he was waiting for her. He had strict ideas about when parties should be over and was one of the world's promptest men. When he said he would come at three o'clock he would always appear at two forty-five.

What a lot of women there were, Cicely thought, who had never learned to drive cars, and quite a few of them were able to press their husbands into service as chauffeurs when the husbands would much rather be out planting apple trees or investigating the habits of muskrats. Such women were notably competent, strong-minded and eloquent.

Cicely admired the skill with which these ladies managed their spouses, but she doubted if she could ever achieve the same effect. Tom was away so often on his architectural affairs that she had had to learn to thaw pipes, put on storm windows, shovel driveways and respond to the thousand and one emergencies that beset the country dweller in the electric age. It was too late in life for her to achieve fragility.

In another century, Tom told her, she would undoubtedly have been driving a covered wagon to California, repelling attacks of Sioux and Shoshone and shooting buffalo. Having driven twice across the continent near one of the emigrant routs and having seen the tracks in the Utah desert worn by the heavy wagons, having crossed Donner Pass and brooded on the disaster of the Donner Party, Cicely often wondered whether she would have had the courage to keep her children alive on a diet of . . . but this line of thought was surely not complimentary to Venetia's delicious luncheon menu.

With the departure of the Countess of Overbrook (Vera Teasdale) on the arm of the Earl (his other arm managing with the deftness of long practice her deck chair, her lapboard and her special cushion) the party swiftly disintegrated until only Cicely was left to assist Venetia in putting away the remains of the meal, and, greatest of pleasures, to talk over the party, which she duly pronounced a success against all Venetia's hesitations about the casserole, her worries over the salad dressing and lamentations as to the height of the layer cake.

Cicely took all these protestations for what they were worth. Not everyone, she knew, purred blandly over the success of a meal in a mood of self-deserved congratulation, as she and her mother often did. Some needed reassurance, so Cicely dealt it out honestly and generously, and at last got Venetia to agree that, yes, everyone did seem to have had a good time.

Menu for a Ladies' Luncheon

For six:

Paella *
Parker House Rolls (p. 122)
Marinated Mushrooms *
Watercress, Avocado, Tomato, Onion Ring Salad
Brownies ‡
Walnut Cake (p. 182)

Paella (V.H.)

For six:

1 fowl, boiled and the meat removed from the bones
2 tablespoons fat from the fowl
4 cups stock from the fowl
2 small onions, minced
meat from 4 pork chops
½ pound pepperoni sausage, skinned and sliced
½ pound rice, washed in 12 changes of water
2 packages of frozen peas or 3 cups fresh peas

½ cup white wine
seasonings: a bit of bay leaf, 4 cloves, salt to taste, pepper from the grinder, ¼ teaspoon powdered saffron, 1 tablespoon chopped parsley
1 can pimentos (4 pimentos), cut in strips
1 pound lobster meat, fresh if possible (or frozen)

This must be made in a large frying pan and brought to the table in the pan.

Cut the pork into small cubes and fry it in the chicken fat till it is tender. Add the onion and cook till it is pale yellow. Add the stock, the white wine, the seasonings (except saffron and parsley) and, when the stock boils, the rice. Add the chicken and cook gently till the rice is done — about 20 minutes. In the meantime, cook the peas. When the rice and peas are ready, sprinkle saffron over the rice and stir it in. Now over the top arrange the pieces of lobster meat, the peas, pimentos and sausage in a handsome red and green design. Sprinkle in the parsley. Cover the pan just long enough to heat the lobster through, and bring to the table amid shrieks of admiration. There are probably as many ways of making this as there are cooks and you might find clams, shrimps, oysters, artichokes or bacon lurking in it here and there. Mrs. Appleyard can vouch for everyone wanting a second round of the above version.

Marinated Mushrooms

Peel and trim 1 pound of small mushrooms. Boil them in water to cover, slightly salted and with the juice of a lemon added. Boil in another saucepan: 1 cup vinegar, half a clove of garlic, 1 bay leaf, a pinch of thyme, 1 teaspoon salt, some freshly ground pepper and 2 spring onions, finely cut. Cool this mixture and take out the garlic. Then add ¾ cup olive oil. Drain the mushrooms well and put them in a deep bowl. Pour the dressing over them and let them stand in it several hours until well chilled and blended. Serve them in a shallow dish, sprinkled with chopped parsley and basil, finely cut.

October

The Bake-Off

It all began with the Surprise Cheesecake. This confection, made according to Mrs. Appleyard's favorite formula, surprised that lady more than anyone. It happened that it was her turn to entertain the croquet players. Naturally she tried to plan the perfect menu. She wanted it to be simple, in a sinister and exotic way, fitting for guests about to engage in this ferocious sport. Yet, she felt, the meal should end with something soothing enough to discourage actual mayhem upon the greensward.

Ice cream seemed too innocent, not to mention a little too

cool for Indian summer. She toyed briefly with the idea of Baked Alaska, as suiting the bitter-sweet, hot-and-cool character of this her favorite season. The oven, however, had recently developed a morose habit of refusing to light and then changing its mind suddenly. Only yesterday it had blown Mrs. Appleyard, that thistledown cook, across the Summer Kitchen and part way into the woodshed. Certainly she would expose neither herself nor a fragile meringue to such temperamental behavior.

"We'll have cheesecake," she told Patience Barlow, handing her a list of ingredients suitable for a safari by the Swiss Family Robinson. "I think we have everything on hand," she added, and got to work on a project concerning Boeuf à la Mode.

By the time she had put the beef away to jelly, the cheesecake emerged from the oven, wreathed in flaky pastry, quivering slightly in the center, brown but not too brown — a handsome sight. As Mrs. Appleyard consumed her sanitary lunch of cold boiled rice garnished with prunes, she wished she could eat about a square foot of cheesecake. Of course she restrained herself. When dessert time came that evening, she was delighted to have several of her guests state that they had never tasted anything like it and ask for the rule. Balls were clicking furiously on the lawn for the final round before she got round to trying it herself.

She had never tasted anything like it either!

This was no ordinary cheesecake, suave, sweet and serene. This was cheesecake with a tang. It had a faint suggestion of Welsh rabbit or of cheese fondue, only with the cool and creamy consistency of cheesecake. It was to ordinary cheesecake, she decided, as Berlioz is to Schubert.

The embattled croquet players, Mrs. Appleyard reflected as

she cut herself another slice, were not the only ones who would like the rule. She'd like it herself . . .

The mystery was explained when she went to get cream for the coffee. The bowl of cottage cheese that ought to have been in the cheesecake was right next to the cream. The fine chunk of Vermont Cheddar, destined for Cheese Soufflé the next day, had vanished. Mrs. Appleyard leaped immediately and correctly to a conclusion about where it was: in the cheesecake, of course, imparting that subtle and racy flavor.

"Nonsense," she said the next morning when Patience Barlow expressed sorrow at the transposition of cheeses, "this is one of the discoveries of the age. We'll enter it in the Sillsbury Bake-off and you shall go to New York, stay at the Waldorf, and win a new gas stove and $25,000. Or anyway a stove," she added prudently, for after all she is a New Englander and therefore subject to these attacks of moderation.

Patience Barlow is even more restrained. She refused to be dazzled by Mrs. Appleyard's lyric description of the new stove. She admitted they could use it, *but* . . .

"I guess you'd better be the one to go," she said firmly.

So that was how Mrs. Appleyard happened to find herself on television, baking cheesecake in a peach-colored stove in a Louis Seize ballroom. There she was in the pale blue smock Patience had made for her. She had on her comfortable shoes, the blue suede ones. She was glad she had bought new laces for them. The extra knots in the old ones had become rather tired looking.

Crystal chandeliers shot spectrums above her head as she deftly blended cheese and cream. She was slightly hampered in her motions by a large spray of white and purple orchids. A young man had just pinned them to her shoulder. He looked like Cary Grant, only smaller, and he had on a pale giraffe-colored linen suit with an orange cummerbund.

"This program is being broadcast in compatible color," he told Mrs. Appleyard. "You should have cherries and chopped chives on your cake."

"What's compatible about that?" Mrs. Appleyard asked, but he had already slithered off and was mounting camellias on a black velvet shoulder. Its owner was baking mushroom short-cake. There were two orchestras competing with the roar of the Waring Blendors. One was playing the part of Berlioz's *Romeo and Juliet* where the young Capulets are going home from the ball. The other was weaving through Schubert's "Trout Quintet." Mrs. Appleyard thought they rather slurred some nuances by eating cucumber sandwiches as they played.

"But I suppose they know best," she said generously.

She put her cake in the oven and joined the croquet game. The wickets, she noticed, were made of spun sugar. Her smallest granddaughter was crawling through one and eating another. This reminded Mrs. Appleyard of another croquet game some-how. Except that there were flamingos in that one and hedge-hogs for balls, which was obviously foolish. These balls were made of popover batter.

"Just sign the receipt," said the Cary Grant young man in the heavy black spectacles, handing her $25,000 in chocolate wrapped in gold, a jade green stove neatly set with emeralds, and a chinchilla apron. "The tax will be $26,000. You can pay as you leave."

Was Mrs. Appleyard glad to wake up and find that it was a Phantom Bake-off? Will she ever get a new gas stove? (The emerald-studded one would have done so nicely for the Princess to make curry on at her next visit.) Will Patience Barlow try

Mrs. Appleyard's idea for Dream of Mushroom Shortcake?

Tune in any time, and if you hear the answers, please let Mrs. Appleyard know.

Surprise Cheesecake

Enough Two-Thousand-Layer pastry to line a 10-inch pie plate.

½ package Lorna Doone short-   ¼ cup melted butter
   bread rolled into fine crumbs

Or — if you have no pastry on hand — use a 9-inch spring form mold and roll fine:

2 packages Lorna Doones and   1 tablespoon Spry for greasing
   use ¾ cup melted butter   mold

For the cheesecake mixture:

½ cup sugar   4 eggs
1½ teaspoons grated lemon rind   3 tablespoons lemon juice
½ cup flour   1½ pounds soft Cheddar cheese
2 8-ounce packages cream   not too mild
   cheese   1 cup heavy cream
          4 ounces blanched almonds

Line the plate with pastry or mix the shortbread crumbs with melted butter. Save out ¾ cup of the crumbs to sprinkle on top of the cake. Grease the spring form mold with Spry and press the rest of the crumb mixture on the bottom and sides of the mold.

Now light the oven — 325°. In the electric mixer beat the eggs at speed 3 until light. Beat in sugar until mixture is creamy, then lemon juice and rind. Then add Cheddar cheese, rather coarsely grated, cream cheese in small lumps. Keep beating and add the flour gradually. Increase speed to 6 (whipping cream) and beat 2 minutes. Add cream. Beat until smooth — about 1 minute. Do not overbeat. Pour into lined plate or mold. Sprinkle with crumb mixture. Decorate with blanched almonds. Bake 1 hour at 325°; turn off the oven and let stand 1 hour longer. Chill well. Serves twelve.

Try and Try Again

C ICELY was always glad that it was to the members of the Book Club that she had decided to serve Croque-bouches. She did have better sense, she hoped, than to try something both new and difficult on a group less generous in spirit. She had seen the recipe for this rare treat in the Sunday magazine section of a reputable newspaper. Its difficulty appeared to lie chiefly in the construction of the pyramid of glazed and filled cream puffs on their base of pastry. The recipes for the various parts did not seem impossible by themselves.

Book Club fell on alternate Thursdays. Perhaps it was partly because Cicely had to produce the program for the evening as well as the refreshments that her attention wandered during the preparation of her *pièce de résistance*. Somehow Sophocles and cream puffs did not mix; Oedipus and puff pastry were antithetical. Thoughts on Greek drama kept drifting between her and the candy thermometer.

She began the Croque-bouches early Thursday morning, intending to set the parts away to be assembled after supper, since the recipe said that it should be served quite soon after it was made. Lucky that she did, for trouble began at once with the pastry base. Cicely had achieved a light hand with yeast dough, but she had never reached the mastery of pastry that her mother and sister possessed. Try as she would, the mixture stuck to the board, the rolling pin and to her, until in frustration she gave the whole grimy mess to Camilla for doll pies and substituted a pastry mix, usually reliable and guaranteed to resist the most brutal treatment.

The resulting pastry base was acceptable, though scarcely of the required thousand-layer variety, and Cicely started on the cream puffs. Some slavish streak made her follow the magazine's recipe for them rather than her own familiar and successful one. She was still doting enough to believe that a newspaper which printed the truth would also have infallible recipes. The low-lying pancakes which greeted her when she opened the oven door were enough to shake the most sanguine soul. When the Bendix with a grinding rattle and groan burned out its main bearing shortly thereafter, Cicely knew that this was one of Those Days.

Grimly she called the plumber and kicked the pile of wash she had planned on finishing that afternoon behind the stove. A second batch of cream puffs were just high enough to admit a knife. This used up all the eggs, since four were reserved for the pastry cream. Hens had recently grown weary of laying, and the store was all out of them till the morning.

She should have known better, Cicely told herself, than to try the pastry cream at all, after this multiple warning. It curdled, and then when she tried to coax it back with more cream it refused to thicken. Fortunately she had a vanilla pudding on the emergency shelf, and by some miracle did not scorch it. After whipped cream had been beaten into it, it looked quite respectable, but of course there would be no mistaking that heavily synthetic flavor of vanilla.

Now for the glaze. The cooking of the sugar syrup coincided with the plumber's arrival — Cicely is one of the few people in Appleyard Center who can send for a plumber and get him the same day; naturally she takes this as a personal tribute — and in the course of visiting with Mr. Harmon in the cellar she let the syrup crystallize when it should have remained golden and syrupy. Of course it is much more important to be on good terms with your plumber than to keep an eye on the candy thermometer, and Mr. Harmon always had a tale or two to tell that she did not like to miss. Thus it was that they were both in the cellar when the boiler sprang a large leak.

Cicely always considered this one of the most fortunate parts of the whole day. Handy though she had become with tools, she could not have staunched so large a leak with chewing gum or electrician's tape. She abandoned the making of syrup till later in the day and gave heed to Mr. Harmon while he explained how long it would take to get the necessary parts from Burlington for the Bendix. The boiler he could replace tomorrow; meanwhile there would be no hot water.

By now Cicely knew that she should never have embarked on so vainglorious a creation as the Croque-bouches, led astray by the fetching name and impressive picture. She made a package angel cake of the sort that is almost impossible to tell from a homemade one, except that it is usually better, and called it a day at the cookstove. The prospect of no hot water for washing up did not encourage her to continue her experiments, so she cooked the crystallized syrup over with water to thin it; not a success, she noted mentally, but it could hardly matter now.

The children's supper was early and sketchy, served from the stove to save dishes. Blessing the invention of television as she settled them in front of the set, Cicely attacked the final assembly of the Croque-bouches. It was worse than she had imagined. The cream puffs had sunk even lower since she took them from the oven and it was all she could do to find room for any of the filling. When she piled them on the pastry base they should ideally have risen like a veritable Matterhorn of crispness; instead they lay limply upon one another like old sponges and what filling had got in promptly ran out. The glaze was thin and weak instead of golden and robust. Finally she had to transfer the whole creation to a bowl instead of the glass platter she had planned to use.

The ladies of the Appleyard Center Book Club were friends indeed that night. They ate the Croque-bouches and even pronounced it good. Cicely had exhibited it more as an object lesson for herself than as part of the refreshments. Happily the rest of the evening made her feel, as always, that she loved the human race and particularly that part of it which had chosen to live within five miles or so of Appleyard Center. Why this was she could never quite say, except that the half-dozen women, some older, some younger than she, who met together during the winter to read poetry or plays, somehow gave each other stimulus, affection and support of a kind that rarely existed between two friends, let alone six or seven.

By the time Cicely had had her second cup of coffee she could feel at one with the world again, not a storm-tossed, star-crossed particle kicked around by the elements, mocked by machines and materials. As a sign that she felt better she took another piece of angel cake. Perhaps after all she would not write that tart letter canceling her subscription to the *Sunday Clarion.*

Cicely feels somewhat bitter still about the Croque-bouches and pettishly refuses to give the rule. Mrs Appleyard has kindly supplied a rule for Cream Puffs that is not stylish, but reliable.

Cream Puffs

No one has ever improved on the classic rule for cream puff batter. Mrs. Appleyard hasn't tried to do so and doesn't intend to, but she has a suggestion about adapting it to modern equipment that she hopes may save you some energy — as it has her. The rule for the batter is, as usual:

½ cup butter	1 cup boiling water
4 eggs	1 cup flour

Bring the water to the boiling point in a quart saucepan. Add the butter immediately. As soon as the mixture boils again dump in the flour all at once. Remove the pan from the heat and stir hard until the mixture leaves the sides of the pan.

There is always a moment when it seems as if it were never going to do this, but be brave — it will. Light the oven — 375°. Now transfer the batter to the large bowl of the electric mixer. Set the dial at the speed for creaming butter. Break the eggs in one at a time, beating half a minute after each addition and scraping the batter in toward the beaters carefully with a rubber scraper, known to Mrs. Appleyard as the Miser's Delight — one of the few items that used to cost ten cents and still does. Beat at least one minute after the last egg is in. Put the batter by spoonfuls on a large cooky sheet. If you have a steady hand and eye you may be able to get a neatly spaced design of twelve puffs. Mrs. Appleyard, to her shame be it said, often ends up with nine, some larger than others. Bake them for half an hour. Then turn the pan so they will bake evenly, reduce the heat to 325°, and bake until there are no iridescent bubbles left on them — about half an hour longer. If you have any doubts, remove the smallest and least symmetrical one and see what happens. If it is not done, it will soon collapse like a weary popover. If it holds its shape, the others can come out too.

The ways of filling them, Mrs. Appleyard generously leaves you to decide for yourself. Her customers usually seem pretty well satisfied with vanilla ice cream inside and chocolate sauce outside. However, just to keep her public mentally active, she has been known to include such substances as crabmeat or lobster salad. She had a caviar and sour cream phase too, small puffs for this. She says her Pâté Maison (p. 213) tastes pretty good in them too.

While she is on the subject of labor-saving in the cream puff zone, she will just mention, her face reddening slightly, that her attempt to make the batter in the electric blender resulted in a catastrophe of considerable proportions. She still bears a scar from contact with one of the knives — so does the Spendthrift's Enemy, the rubber scraper. This was incurred in the line of duty while extricating a certain amount of a very adhesive mixture. The puffs turned out to be an exercise of making molehills out of mountains but the bluejays were crazy about the result. So never mind!

Menus for a Reading Circle

Angel Cake with Raspberry Cream*
Coffee

Apple Pie with Ice Cream*
Tea or Sanka

Oatmeal Shortbread*
Hot Chocolate

Orange Bread*
Fruit Punch

Shortbread*
Chocolate Crisps*

Cicely's friends are not only sympathetic and supporting in time of disaster, sympathetic and jubilant in time of triumph. They are good cooks too. The menus to accompany literary evenings were contributed by them. She leaves the reader to decide whether the angel cake or the apple pie goes better with Chekhov, the oatmeal shortbread or the orange nutbread with Sophocles. All she does is to warn you that coffee on top of *Hamlet* can lead to a thoroughly sleepless night.

Angel Cake with Raspberry Cream (E.B.F.)

1 Angel Food Cake (see p. 33), sliced horizontally in thirds. Dissolve 1 package plain gelatin in ¼ cup cold water. Bring to a boil the juice of 2 packages frozen raspberries and add to the dissolved gelatin. Put the berries in the mixture, place in refrigerator and allow to stiffen. Whip ½ pint heavy cream and fold into the gelatin mixture. Spread the mixture between the layers and on top and sides of the cake. Serve right away.

Apple Pie with Ice Cream (E.C.H.)

Pastry: For a 9-pie dish

2 cups Gold Medal sifted flour
1 teaspoon salt
⅔ cup and 2 tablespoons shortening — Fluffo if you like a golden
  look to the pastry, otherwise Crisco
4 tablespoons water

Filling:

7 cups sliced apples —   1 cup sugar and 1 teaspoon cin-
  Wealthys are good   namon

Dot with 1½ tablespoons butter and bake the pie at 425° for 50–60 minutes. Serve with a scoop of ice cream on each piece.

Oatmeal Shortbread (S.P.M.)

3½ cups oatmeal
⅔ cup sugar
¼ cup flour

1¼ sticks butter or margarine
½ teaspoon salt
1 teaspoon vanilla

Work all ingredients together in a bowl. Have 9 x 13 x 2 pan thoroughly floured and buttered. Put mixture into pan and press down firmly. Bake in moderate oven (325°) about 30 minutes or till lightly browned. Remove from oven and cool about 10 minutes. Cut into squares.

Scotch Shortbread (P.B.H.)

½ cup confectioners' sugar
1 cup butter
2 cups sifted bread flour

¼ teaspoon salt
¼ teaspoon baking powder

Cream the butter, add the sugar and blend thoroughly. Mix salt and baking powder with flour, sift again. Blend with the creamed mixture by hand till thoroughly mixed. Roll ⅓

inch thick. Prick all over with a fork. Bake on a greased sheet 20 minutes at 375° or until delicately brown. If you have them available, press the mixture into small Swedish molds, prick and bake.

Chocolate Crisps (P.B.H.)

1 package Nestlé semi-sweet chocolate bits or your favorite brand

2 cups Kelloggs' K cereal (full of protein)

Melt chocolate in top of double boiler. Remove from the stove, add K cereal. Stir in carefully. Shape teaspoonfuls on wax paper. Chill at least half an hour. You might add ½ teaspoonful instant coffee for the sake of variety.

Orange Bread (E.H.D.)

3 cups sifted flour
1½ cups sugar
3 teaspoons baking powder
1 cup ground orange rind

3 tablespoons butter
1 egg
1 cup milk

Simmer the orange rind in water to cover. When tender, remove white part and grind the remainder in food chopper. Make the batter in the usual way, but let it stand ½ hour before putting into oven. Bake in a loaf pan at 350° for 1 hour and 20 minutes.

Last Party of the Season

I<small>T IS</small> a common delusion on the part of summer visitors to Appleyard Center that when they go away life stops. Actually, of course, from the point of view of the winter residents, life begins. It refreshes their spirits to know that they are no longer referred to as "natives" by — if one judges by those brightly flowered skirts and shirts, those fluttering scarves, those clanking beads and bracelets — peasants from Lower Scythia.

Neatly and fashionably dressed in their basic black dresses, their charcoal-gray suits, Vermonters carry on their own lives. They raise money for the Red Cross and the March of Dimes. They buy shining cars, larger and handsomer cars than the out-of-state vehicles they have been pulling out of ditches all summer.

They stop pasteurizing milk and begin reading books from the Book Wagon. They organize Chicken Pie Suppers and variety shows for the benefit of the Hot Lunch Program. They drive fifty miles over frozen ruts, through sleet and slush, and down ice-glazed hills to listen to the Vermont Symphony. A good many of them go to Florida, where they take a kindly interest in quaint native customs of which they will have good stories to tell when they get back, come cowslip time.

Mrs. Appleyard knows all these things, for she sometimes invades the winter privacy of the hills. She realizes that when she goes away she takes with her just her own life, not anyone else's. Still, as she hides the key in the usual place, sees Roger Willard taking in the mailbox, hears the gate click behind her, looks back at the weathered blue shutters so neatly closed, even she feels that parties are over. Naturally she is wrong.

Before she has crossed the Connecticut, the mice have given a series of small exclusive dances in her miniature rooms. In the Salem dining room, the one with the lacquer cabinets and the Chinese rug, they have knocked over three Queen Anne chairs, a candlestand and a silver bowl of fruit. In the Vermont room there is pewter on the floor. There would be cider too if there had been a quarter of a teaspoonful in the cider jug.

Refreshments consisting of flowers from the garden outside the French windows were served in the living room of the Great Porcupine Island house. As usual one domestically inclined mouse has tried to take up knitting again. She has already been into Mrs. Appleyard's pantry to pick out a suitable ice-cream cone for a bassinette. She has no better luck than usual at finishing that baby blanket and the ball of wool — as usual — is under the maple bed in the room with the stenciled walls.

Menus for Frosty Evenings

As Mrs. Appleyard does not have access to the mouse family's private manuscript cookbooks and file of appropriate menus she offers some of those she uses herself at this season.

Broiled Flounder Fillets* with Lemon Butter*
Broiled Tomatoes*
Shell Beans and Mushrooms*
Popovers
Apricot Almond Trifle*

Pâté Casa Blanca*   Melba Toast
Risotto*
Tomato Sauce*
Onion Relish*
Autumn Garden Salad
Apple Pie with a Tang*
Coffee   Red Wine

Porterhouse Steak, Planked*
Mashed Potatoes
Broiled Tomatoes (p. 211) and Mushrooms
Fried Onions
Yorkshire Pudding*
Prunes in Jelly*
Brownies‡

Broiled Flounder Fillets

Allow 2 fillets for each person. Squeeze lemon juice over them, paint them with a pastry brush with melted butter. Do this on both sides and fold them neatly. Do not roll them: they should lie flat. Lay them in a shallow buttered pan and slide it under the broiler. Broil on both sides until they are delicately brown, about 3 minutes on each side, but this will depend on the thickness of the fillets, distance from the flame and your broiler. They should not dry out, but be thoroughly cooked, yet tender. Remove to a hot platter and spread over them the following sauce. For six fillets:

Lemon Butter

¼ cup butter
grated rind of 1 lemon
2 tablespoons lemon juice

1 teaspoon chopped parsley
1 teaspoon chopped chives

1 teaspoonful of your favorite fresh herbs, minced (Mrs. Appleyard likes small amounts of chervil, tarragon, thyme and basil, but choose your own)

Cream the butter, add the lemon juice, rind and herbs. Mix well. Do not melt it. Let the hot fish do that.

Broiled Tomatoes

After the first frost has come it is a pretty sight to see the window sills of white houses decorated with ripening tomatoes rescued the night before.

Now there is the problem of what to do with them. Small, almost ripe ones are good cut in halves, the ends sliced off so they will rest evenly on the pan and broiled. Make some garlic butter. Combine it with fine bread crumbs. Cover the tomatoes rather thickly with the mixture; dust over some grated cheese. Slide the pan under the broiler and cook till the cheese is melted and the crumbs start to brown.

Shell Beans and Mushrooms

One of the happy coincidences of life in Vermont is that in years when there are mushrooms they appear just about when the shell beans, the ones with the carmine splotches on the pods, are ripe.

For six people allow:

2 cups beans, after shelling	1 tablespoon flour
1 pound mushrooms, caps only	1 cup light cream
1 onion, minced	½ cup mushroom stock
2 tablespoons butter	

Seasonings to taste — Mrs. Appleyard uses a little freshly ground pepper and ¼ teaspoonful nutmeg.

This is better to fix ahead of time as it benefits by standing awhile and blending. Cook the beans until they are almost done, about 25 minutes. Start the onion cooking in the butter slowly, until it is pale yellow. Peel and slice the mushrooms. Put on the stems and skins to simmer in hot water. Add the sliced mushroom to the onion and cook until both are tender. Sprinkle in the flour and seasonings and blend them with the butter. Turn off the heat. Blend the cream in carefully. Pretty soon the beans will be cooked. Add any water left in them to the mushroom stock and cook it down to half a cup. If you have been saving a little beef or chicken stock this is a good place to put it. Add the beans to the mushroom mixture. Add the mushroom stock when it is ready. Set the pan aside. Reheat the mixture just before you serve it.

Apricot Almond Trifle

12 ladyfingers, split	4 ounces almonds, blanched
1 cup apricot pulp, sweetened	and peeled
1 cup sugar	1 cup thin cream
3 eggs	2 tablespoons soft butter
1 teaspoon almond extract	2 tablespoons candied fruits,
	diced

Split the ladyfingers and spread them with the sweetened apricot pulp. Put them in a glass bowl in which you will serve the trifle. Put the blanched and peeled almonds into the electric blender. Add the cream and run the blender until the almonds are finely cut. Add the sugar, eggs, flavoring and run until the mixture begins to thicken. Add the butter in small pieces and run the blender until everything is well blended. The mixture should be like thick custard. Pour it over the ladyfingers and decorate the top with candied fruit. Chill the trifle in the refrigerator for several hours.

Mrs. Appleyard has varied this by arranging apricot rolls (p. 172) in between the ladyfingers and by adding toasted almonds to the top decoration just before serving.

She says that the blender is a convenience, not a necessity. The almonds can of course be chopped by hand and the rest of the mixture may be done simply with an egg beater, or an electric mixer.

Pâté Casa Blanca

It was a bright October day, the kind of day Mrs. Appleyard would have said it would not have been possible to improve. This one, however, was made even more memorable than usual by the gift of some wild ducks. Mrs. Appleyard promptly cooked them according to the method advised by the donor. They were allowed to glance at the fire briefly and only the breasts were eaten. Fortunately the next day was cold, dank and dingy — just the right day to stay indoors and make pâté.

Mrs. Appleyard began by taking the meat off the carcasses and cutting it into small neat cubes. She put the bones, the livers and gizzards on to cook in cold water with a carrot, a branch of celery, two onions, herbs and spices. She says the quantities of the seasonings should not be large but she likes several kinds: small pinches of cinnamon, nutmeg and allspice, three cloves, three *chile tepines*, a minute piece of bayleaf, a very little oregano, rosemary and marjoram. Peppercorns may be added during the last 10 minutes. This simmered for 3 hours, during which time Mrs. Appleyard stenciled a tray she had been planning to restore to life ever since she first noticed it in 1912. Apparently she has some tortoise ancestry back somewhere in her pedigree.

When the tray had progressed to a stage where its original owner might possibly have recognized it, the remaining scraps of meat had fallen from the bones and the broth had cooked down to 2 cups. The stock was chilled. This was the kind of day you could chill anything just by setting it outside on the porch table. While it was cooling, Mrs. Appleyard chopped the scraps of meat, liver, gizzard, two chicken livers she had saved for just such an emergency, and a pound of Colburn's Montpelier sausage meat all together. She also rolled out dry Pepperidge Farm bread into crumbs. Somewhere about this time she remembers eating some lukewarm rice and four prunes.

By this time the stock had jellied and the fat had risen to the top. She skimmed off the fat and carefully coated an oven-proof bread pan with it; then dusted fine crumbs all over the fat. She states that she had a cup and a quarter of crumbs and that they were as fine as sand from the Sahara. Three quarters of a cup of crumbs, the jellied broth and two well-beaten eggs were then added to the meat. Last of all she added a small onion chopped very fine, almost to a pulp, and the cubes of duck, mixing them well into the mixture. She added in a wistful tone that she would have put in truffles if she had any.

She lighted the oven — 250° — put the mixture into the pan, coated the top of it with the remaining ¼ cup of Sahara bread crumbs, dotted it with the rest of the duck fat, covered the dish with chef's foil, and set it on a rack in a pan of hot water in the oven. She baked it 3 hours.

During this period she put her feet up and read a good book. (*The Eustace Diamonds* by Anthony Trollope, in case you were thinking of asking; has no opinion as to whether Trollope would have liked the pâté. Standish Appleyard did and that is endorsement enough.)

"You had better list the ingredients," said that gentleman. "I might feel like making one sometime."

Mrs. Appleyard, delighted with this display of interest, did so:

½ cup cubed duck meat	2 cups jellied stock
1 cup minced duck meat, liver, gizzard	2 chicken livers (raw)
	1¼ cups fine bread crumbs
1 carrot, 2 onions, 1 branch celery	2 eggs
herbs and spices, your own assortment, small amounts	1 small onion finely minced or grated

Risotto

There are as many ways of making risotto as there are combinations of things in the icebox. You might, for instance, find:

3 chicken livers	half a can of pimento
a cup of chicken stock	a few mushrooms
half a green pepper	1½ cups cooked rice

Mrs. Appleyard hopes you also have two onions, and some parsley. Start heating the rice in the chicken stock while you mince the onion and slice the pepper, pimento and mushrooms. If you have chicken fat on hand cook the onion in it until it is golden brown, or use butter. Then add the pepper, pimento and mushrooms and cook them until they are tender. If you have a little chicken and a few green beans you may add them to the rice at this point. Now mince the parsley. Add the contents of the frying pan to the rice mixture. Cook the livers in a little more chicken fat or butter. Cut them into small pieces and add them to the rice. Sprinkle the parsley over it before you bring it to the table. The whole process has taken about 15 minutes and the icebox is gratifyingly neat. The risotto will not be correct unless the rice has absorbed the stock so that it is neither wet nor dry — just nicely moist.

Tomato Sauce
(To go with Fish or Meat)

1 pint tomatoes, peeled and chopped, measured after chopping
1 clove of garlic

2 onions, sliced
1 green pepper, minced
2 tablespoons minced chives
salt and pepper to taste

Put the tomatoes, their juice, the onion and the garlic into the electric blender. Run the blender until the tomatoes are well puréed. Strain out the seeds. Add the pepper, chives and seasonings. Serve cold.

Onion Relish (V.H.)

1 medium onion, sliced
grated rind and juice 1 lemon

2 teaspoons sugar
pepper from the grinder

Mix together and let stand one hour before serving. Good with cold meat, hamburg, broiled fish.

Apple Pie with a Tang and Cross Bars

Of course no apple pie is better than the classic kind — light flaky pastry enclosing tart New England apples newly picked, sugar just darkened with cinnamon, nutmeg, 2 cloves, a whisper of grated lemon rind, and a few dots of butter. Still, when there are no apples left and you come across a package in the freezer that says "Dutchess Apples in Syrup" you might like to try this.

She makes the pastry beforehand (p. 93) and puts it into the refrigerator to chill while she is thawing out the apples. Mrs. Appleyard believes this is an illustration of a law of thermodynamics. Something about everything getting to be the same temperature. Naturally such speculations should not keep you, if you have to use apples with their skins on, from peeling, coring and slicing seven or eight of them and poaching them until soft but not mushy in the following syrup:

½ cup sugar
¼ cup water
4 tablespoons maple syrup

Cool slightly and add 1 tablespoon lemon juice, 1 tablespoon orange juice, grated rind of 1 lemon and 1 orange, 1 tablespoon orange cordial. (Mrs. Appleyard makes this by pouring brandy over thin orange peel and adding sugar. You could also get it out of a bottle.)

Now put the seasoned apples into a baking dish and put the crust on in strips. Finish the edge with a ribbon of pastry made by twisting two strips together. Bake at 450° for 15 minutes and then reduce to 350° and bake until the pastry is well browned — about 20 minutes longer.

Porterhouse Steak, Planked

Mrs. Appleyard is the fortunate owner of an oak plank big enough to hold a steak of noble proportions, a wall of mashed potato and a rug of vegetables. However, the plank is not really necessary. The various items can be cooked separately and arranged around any platter large enough to hold them comfortably and leave room for carving the steak. There are also aluminum well-and-tree pans that go right under the broiler and can be set on a larger platter for serving.

However you serve it, it is still steak and should be treated with respect. Mrs. Appleyard does not respect any steak less than two inches thick. There are, of course, different tastes about steak. If you like yours well browned outside and tender, juicy and reddish pink inside, here is how Mrs. Appleyard achieves that purpose whether the steak is planked or merely broiled. She cooks partly by ear. A steak not only looks and smells done but it sounds done, she says. There is a certain vibrant purposeful hiss and fizz from a steak that is ready to eat. Listen for it and train your ear to it.

To keep the juice where it belongs, inside the steak, instead of letting it run out and dry up, Mrs. Appleyard begins by searing it on both sides. The searing time depends somewhat on the size of the steak — that is, its whole area, its thickness, its temperature. For a large steak, one weighing somewhere near three pounds, cool from the refrigerator (not the freezer) she allows two minutes on each side. By the time it is seared on both sides she knows by sight, smell and sound how long the rest of the cooking will take. As she turns it back to the first side she is usually heard to say in her crystal ball tone: "This needs five minutes on the first side and four on the second," or some such occult remark based on a mysterious type of inferential calculus, and then she adds crisply: "Platter ready at seven-five."

In figuring when the steak will be ready to serve she includes the time spent turning it. A clock with a moving second hand is a great help, she says.

The schedule for a 2¾-pound steak will run about like this.

Close to the flame:
      Side A: 2 minutes
      Turning: 1 minute
      Side B: 2 minutes
      Turning: 1 minute
Slightly farther from the flame:
      Side A: 5 minutes
      Turning: 1 minute
      Side B: 4 minutes

      Transfer to platter: 2 minutes
      Total time: 18 minutes

Please note that Side B will always receive just a little less time than side A. That is because it actually received some cooking from the heated broiler underneath, although it is side A that first faces the flame. If you expose side B as long as side A, your steak will be overcooked. If you get into the habit of listening to it while it cooks you will hear that this is so as well as taste it later.

This schedule is for any steak. For one to be served on a plank the principle is the same up to the second cooking of side B. At this point you transfer the steak, turning side B uppermost, to your well-oiled plank. Quickly heap fluffy mashed potato around the edge and arrange in between it and the steak mushroom caps dotted with butter, sliced tomatoes already partly cooked and covered with buttered crumbs, little heaps of partly fried onions. This will take at least five minutes and as your steak cannot help losing a little cooking momentum you will probably have to give it five minutes under the broiler instead of four for a plain steak. This would make a five-minute difference in the total time, which would then be 23 minutes instead of 18.

However, since no two steaks are exactly alike, this is only, Mrs. Appleyard says, a slightly more definite guide than any she was ever given. The great thing is to train your ear to know when the steak is done as *you* like it and to be sure that each side gets two turns at the flame. Mrs. Appleyard thinks a steak, either plain or planked, looks handsomest with plenty of crisply curled parsley around it.

Spanish Steak Sauce

Cicely cannot resist putting in her favorite sauce for steak: Melt half a cup of butter in the broiler pan after you cook the steak. Blend 1 tablespoon ketchup, 1 tablespoon paprika, ½ teaspoon mustard and ½ teaspoon sugar in a cup. Add this to the melted butter, also a clove of pricked garlic. As the sauce begins to bubble — you have put the pan on a burner on medium heat — turn down the heat, remove the garlic and add 2 teaspoons vinegar, stir vigorously and remove from the stove at once or it will separate. Serve at once with the steak.

Yorkshire Pudding

Mrs. Appleyard used to think that you couldn't have Yorkshire Pudding unless you had roast beef. Suddenly it dawned on her one wakeful night when she was brooding on various subjects, that this was not necessarily so. Serve it with hamburg, she says: it needs it more than roast beef does and you have your oven free to bake it at just the right temperature. Also she says that you can make it better in the electric blender or the electric mixer than you can by hand. She saves beef fat from a roast or steak or gets a little suet from the butcher and tries it out. This she puts into a nine-inch heavy iron enameled frying pan so that it is half an inch deep. The batter is the traditional one:

1 cup milk	1 cup flour
3 eggs, well beaten	salt to taste

Light the oven — 400°. Add the milk slowly to the flour sifted four times, beating as you do it. Beat the eggs in one at a time. (In the electric blender you dump everything in and whizz! It's done!)

Bake until it is well risen — 15 to 20 minutes. Reduce the heat to 300° and bake 15 minutes longer when it should be light, crisp and a pleasing deep amber in color.

Prunes in Jelly

½ pound quick-cooking prunes	grated rind 1 lemon
¼ pound almonds, blanched	2 cups juice from prunes (hot)
2 envelopes plain gelatin	½ cup cold water
½ cup lemon juice	¼ cup sherry
¼ cup sugar	

Cook the prunes until they are tender and the pits can be easily removed. Substitute a blanched almond for each pit. Arrange the rest of the almonds at the bottom of heat-proof glass custard cups which have been rinsed out with cold water. Soak the gelatin in cold water ten minutes. Add the hot prune juice. It should be almost boiling. If you haven't enough, add boiling water. Stir well. Cool slightly. Add the sugar, lemon juice, rind, and sherry. If you do not care for sherry, substitute orange juice or water. Taste it. Add more sugar if you like it very sweet. Pour a little of the liquid into each mold. Let it cool until it begins to set, then pack in the prunes. Pour in the rest of the liquid. Chill in the refrigerator. Serve with the kind of Vermont cream that is so annoying that you have to get it out of the jar with a spoon.

Variation: Use apricots instead of prunes. Increase the sugar to ⅔ cup. More if you like it very sweet.

The Summer Kitchen

It's high time," said Mrs. Appleyard rather sternly to her daughter, "that you got your part of this book written."

She was speaking on the telephone to Cicely at the time and as they were a couple of hundred miles apart and it was midnight or thereabouts they were having a comfortable uninterrupted conversation of a sort that was quite impossible at closer quarters or during the day. Anyone who thinks Vermonters are a taciturn race had better try getting the line after the dishes are done any morning in the week.

"I know," said Cicely. "I wish I were a stronger character. I need something to set me off."

A few weeks later Cicely received a firm but kindly note saying that the manuscript for *The Summer Kitchen* should be finished in two weeks' time. As she was due to leave for New York the next morning where she had, in a moment of giddy courage, undertaken to show the city to thirty-one adolescents including, worst folly of all, her own eldest daughter, she was not in a position to write any books that week.

By the time she got home it was May. The sort of controlled chaos usually characteristic of her establishment had got a little out of hand. The caretaking young couple had broiled steaks in the fireplace and dropped them on the new floor along with their cups of coffee — that, at least, was Cicely's archaeological research. Two lambs had been born and one had died. The other had to have its tail removed, a problem handily solved by the use of a cutter for chewing tobacco. Tommy Bradshaw had bought it at an auction three years before, saying that it would come in handy. Cynthia needed a dress for a dance so Cicely spent an evening sewing, winding up with hemming a skirt four yards around. This left her cross-eyed the next day, a poor state for typing.

Carpenters and plumbers drifted in and out, engaged in remodeling the kitchen. Cicely discovered that if she shut herself away upstairs in a quiet room she suffered more interruptions than if she stayed downstairs where she could be easily consulted about the proper position of windows and appliances. Also the children could more easily ask her for something to eat when they got home from school and she could more briskly tell them to go and open a can of soup. During the writing of so elegant a cookbook the meals at Sky Farm consisted largely of hot dogs scorched on the gas burners, brownies, cold cereal, potato chips, popsicles, fudge and raw carrots.

The table on which she wrote was within happy hearing

distance of the television set. Occasionally she would find that she had written Honolulu for Hamburger or fabulous for frying pan as certain voices penetrated the veil of concentration that she was able most of the time to maintain between herself and the real world. On the table curious still-life formations began to collect. Over and under the recipes, carbon paper, filing cards and scraps of yellow paper essential to the book, drifted teddy bears and newspapers, coffee cups and fish hooks, unsorted laundry and report cards, patterns for ballet costumes, unread magazines, unpaid bills, saltines and binoculars.

"If only . . . " Cicely would begin to complain to her hardhearted co-author. "If only Tommy hadn't had to go to the hospital with mysterious spots, I should have been finished yesterday. I feel like a prisoner."

"Nonsense," said her mother briskly. "You know you prefer it this way. If it wasn't Tommy's spots it would be somebody's tonsils. Have you written about the Covered-Dish Supper yet?"

"Camilla was singing all this morning — 'Come down from your ivory tower — come down from your ivory tower.' What do you suppose she meant?" Cicely asked.

"Don't change the subject," admonished her mother. "I shall be up Saturday so you had better get into high gear. Your work habits are deplorable, but I love you just the same." And she hung up, feeling as usual that there was something faintly vicious about long-distance telephoning.

I will finish on Mother's Day, said Cicely to herself. Sunday is a nice quiet day and I can work all the time. Meanwhile Mrs. Appleyard supplied her with page after page of beautifully illegible manuscript which only the two of them could decipher.

On Sunday Cicely began the day by going to clean the

church. She had forgotten that it was her turn. Then she had to arrange for the sheep to go to be sheared. Next there were cupcakes to be made for the farewell tea for the minister and his wife. She overestimated the size of the pans and all the lids came off, so she stuck them together with frosting and called them filled cookies. Camilla had a nosebleed and came dripping through the hall.

"Go away, you Stone Age woman," she said to Cicely. "You wish I was dead."

It was time to go to choir practice. Bach made her feel better but it didn't get her further on with her typing. The farewell tea went smoothly. There were enough cupcakes without Cicely's. Her daffodils shared in the decorations. She sniffled happily during the speeches. This was one of the days on which she loved everybody. If only . . .

Sunday was going fast. The pile of typed sheets grew higher. Mrs. Appleyard and Venetia Hopkins invited Cicely to supper.

"I can eat or type," she said, "but not both."

She accepted on the grounds that a last consultation was needed. This produced, as she feared, seven more recipes to type out. The manuscript had got into the dangerous stage in which the two authors kept writing in remarks to each other not originally intended for publication.

"This must stop," said Cicely, and she piled her various papers into a cardboard box and went home. A moon as thin as a shaving hung impossibly large above her yellow house, looking like a Hollywood-scale sign for a New Moon Café.

As she typed the last words of the last section of the last chapter the telephone rang. It was Cynthia. She wished to be fetched home from where she was visiting. Also she had seen a bathing suit she needed terribly. Everybody was buying a bathing suit.

"Won't you even discuss it?" Cynthia asked.

"No," said Cicely suddenly. "This is *Mother's* Day. And I'm coming down from my ivory tower." She hung up before Cynthia could reply, laid the last sheets of manuscript on the proper pile and began to sort the laundry. The cat asked to be let in and the dog to be let out.

How difficult it is to be literary, she thought. Life keeps breaking in. Or is it out? (Luckily it's both, says Mrs. Appleyard.)

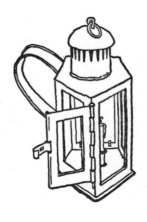

Index